IT's IN THE BAG

A REVOLUTION IN PET TRAVEL
GAYLE MARTZ

IT's IN THE BAG

A REVOLUTION IN PET TRAVEL
GAYLE MARTZ

Favorite Quotes, and One of My Own

When I look into the eyes of an animal I do not see an animal.
I see a living being. I see a friend. I feel a soul.

— *A.D. Williams*

I have found that when you are deeply troubled, there are
things you get from the silent devoted companionship
of a dog that you can get from no other source.

— *Doris Day*

Dogs come into our lives to teach us about love.
They depart to teach us about loss. A new dog
never replaces an old dog, it merely expands the heart.

— *Erica Jong*

You will never replace or forget a dog's unconditional love
and spirit as they change and enrich our lives forever.

—*Gayle Martz*

Dedication

*This book is dedicated to my beloved mother, Connie.
Your belief in me, your steadfast support as a
business partner and best friend, were the
foundation on which I built SHERPA.*

*I also dedicate this book to all my fellow animal
lovers and my four legged muse, SHERPA,
and to all those who helped me grow the
SHERPA brand, as industry partners, colleagues,
best friends, vendors and customers.
Thank you all from the bottom of my heart!*

It's in the Bag!
A Revolution in Pet Travel

Library of Congress Cataloguing-in-Publication Data

ISBN 978-0-9883591-6-1

1. Inspirational memoirs
2. Entrepreneurship and Business
3. Brand Building
4.Travel with Pets

Published by New Voices Press
Collaborating Writer Judith Katz,

Editorial consultant Kai Flanders

Copy and research assistance by Christian Luehmann

Book interior design by Tony Iatridis,
InnovationDesignGraphics.com

Cover Art by Cynthia Neilson

Table of Contents

Chapter 1

From the Depths of Despair, Dream Big

O n a crisp October evening in 2019, I was doing the thing that makes me feel the proudest of anything in the world: taking a flight with one of my dogs. If you don't know me or my story, that might sound like a strange thing to be proud of. Almost anyone can fly with a pet onboard these days. Well, let me say with all modesty, it's precisely *because* of me that you can.

On this particular flight, I was going from Paris to New York with my beloved Shih Tzu, KARTU, safe and comfortable underneath the seat in front of me in her SHERPA Bag. It was one of the many styles in my line of soft-sided SHERPA pet carriers. KARTU was allowed the privilege of being such a jet-setter largely due to the pet travel revolution that began when I founded my own company, Gayle Martz Inc. and under that umbrella created my first "DBA" (doing business as) SHERPA Pet Trading Company in 1989—a revolution I have continued to champion for three decades. Helping pets travel in safety, comfort, and style has been my life's work and legacy.

As the plane began its descent, I saw the glowing outline of Manhattan rise into view, and I felt a flutter in my stomach. It wasn't nervousness—I've spent much of my adult life in the sky, both as a passenger and a flight attendant for TWA Airlines. It was the thrill of anticipation. I was excited to be heading to The Silver Wings International convention, which was going to be held in the newly built TWA Hotel at John F. Kennedy Airport. The Silver Wings, an organization founded by a group of retired

1

TWA flight attendants to celebrate the pride and dignity of their chosen profession, had invited over a thousand of us to have a giant "layover" at the airline-themed hotel. I was more than ready to see old friends, reminisce about missed connections and bumpy flights, exchange a bit of gossip, and take a myriad of photos.

When the plane was safely on the ground, I scooped up KARTU in her SHERPA Bag and headed for Terminal 5. There I found a giant red and white elevator with the words "TWA Hotel" emblazoned across its doors. It was a bit strange but good to not have to leave the airport to arrive at my lodgings.

A giant red hallway opened up to one of the most interesting hotel lobbies I'd ever seen, and I've stayed in more than my fair share of hotels. It took me a moment to realize that it was a revamped version of the original TWA Flight Center Terminal, which was originally built in 1962. I was hired by the company in 1970, so I was very familiar with this territory. There was an exact replica of Jack Frye's office, the most beloved president in company history. His favorite drink, a scotch on the rocks, sat on his *actual* desk from 1934. They even had the old arrivals and departures board with the numbers ticking away. Massive windows with sweeping vistas looked out at an actual TWA propeller plane.

After getting my room keys, I went to the registration room to go collect my convention credentials. On the way, I passed a display of flight attendant uniforms from the 1940s to the 1990s. To my delight, I spied the one I stood in for my graduation from the TWA academy in 1971, including the white gloves. These days, flight attendants certainly don't wear gloves.

At the registration desk, I got my laminated ID and looked around to see if anyone I knew was checking in. My eyes landed on three women; all three were holding SHERPA Bags. That wasn't too unusual: I see my bags in airports all the time, which is one of my great pleasures, but these bags looked brand new. They still had the tags on them. Then another woman walked over, holding up her bag, and said, "Gayle Martz! Look what I found." She was someone I knew from our days in the sky.

"So good to see you," I said. "Where exactly did you find that bag?"

"At the TWA store. I just had to have it, and my dog will love it."

"Wonderful! Thank you. Can you tell me where that shop is?"

She pointed me in the right direction, and off I went, KARTU in tow. Sure enough, there were my bags beautifully displayed on a table in the registration room. I watched in glee as a woman picked one up, smiled to herself, and headed to the register. I had no idea that TWA was going to be selling my bags at the convention. I felt like I was a part of history to be included so visibly in this living museum to air travel. This solidified my being a part of the future, as people continued to buy my bags and board planes with their pets safely and comfortably inside.

Over the next several days, over a thousand flight attendants from all over the world filled the hotel. We had amazing dinners, told raucous stories over drinks, and listened to fantastic speakers. Mostly we so enjoyed seeing each other and being together. I felt like a social butterfly, moving around the convention room during events, taking pictures, talking, and listening to tales of days long past.

So many people told me how proud they were that I had done something so meaningful with my life. One woman came up to me and said, "I remember when we were flying on the Lockheed 1011. We were on the jump seat in the galley and while the passengers were sleeping you were sketching the SHERPA Bag. You didn't know that was what you were going to call it then. All you said was, "I'm going to make these."

I gave her a giant hug. Stories like that reminded me of

the reality of life in the 1970s and 80s. Things weren't easy for women back then, and let's be honest—most flight attendants were women back then, but we sure had each other's backs. You had to love people. You had to be able to smile. You had to be able to work very hard over long hours. You didn't complain. You didn't gripe. You made the best of every single moment. When you're surrounded with people like that, there's always those twin blessings of humor and camaraderie.

After I started SHERPA, flight attendants were some of my best advertisers. Even though they weren't transporting their own pets while working, they would carry my bags through airports so people would see them and buy the bags at the luggage stores in the terminal. Worked like a charm. I *always* made sure to give my colleagues a "flight attendant discount" on my products.

After the convention ended and we had all drifted back to our separate corners of the world, I reflected on how being a flight attendant, though only one stage of my life's long journey had been such an important one.

For more than thirty years my mission in life, to ensure that all of us could be able to take our pets with us wherever we go, has taken me all over the world. I have worked with and continue to meet with communities of animal lovers, regulatory and compliance groups, legislators, corporate leaders, and business entities, all designed to increase pet friendly policies and services. I speak at trade shows and give media interviews on how to ensure the safety and comfort of pets when folks travel with them. I've written articles and Op Eds on pet safety and travel with airlines, automotive industry and hotels. It's all part of the goal I've been committed to for the last thirty-three years. In fact, my mantra, which is also the title of my first book, *No Pet Left Behind. I* know how painful leaving your dog or cat behind can be, and often how unnecessary!

Through the years, my mind has been filled with poignant thoughts of SHERPA's business history--a cornucopia of memories from unlimited hours spent building a global brand. There was the joy of traveling on a plane with one of my dogs in the passenger cabin for the very first time. Likewise, there were sweet memories of connecting with a wonderful community of animal lovers worldwide that believe in being able to take their pets with them everywhere they go. At the same time there were also lessons learned and cautionary tales in many situations I experienced as a fledgling entrepreneur, including how to move forward in business and in life when faced with total betrayal.

I have known for more than thirty years that I needed to articulate those memories into a book: the book you now hold in your hands. I decided I needed to tell the whole story of SHERPA. It is a story filled with struggle, complications, victories, and, ultimately, hard-won, hopefully instructive lessons on what it takes to build a company from the ground up. Starting out, I was armed with fierce determination but little else—no home, no money, no job, I did not have the tools I need to build a brand. And yet, against all odds, I did it. If I can, so can others. It is a story I hope people from all walks of life especially those who want to grow a successful business can take to heart and learn from.

Whether you are a man or a woman, I hope my story shows you how to be powerful in the face of all odds, and make your own way, even, as I did, in a male-dominated industry. For entrepreneurs, my story is intended to provide you with key business lessons I hope will serve you well in the inevitable ups and downs of your business venture, or your plan to raise your position in a corporate environment. Most of all, if you are a pet-lover as you must surely be if you are reading this book, I hope you feel comforted and supported by all the others, who, like me and you, want the world to become a better, safer, more accommodating place for our animals. We know how much and how little they ask in return.

My hope is that my telling the story of SHERPA will continue, the *evolution,* of the *revolution* I started all those years ago, and that you, my dear reader, are inspired to help evolve and carry this momentum into the future.

Fittingly, I think, the story of SHERPA begins with another kind of revolution: a strike.

May 1986

As I marched with my fellow flight attendants outside the Trans World Airlines terminal at John F. Kennedy Airport in New York, we held up placards with slogans like *Flight Attendants Are Breadwinners Too!* And *I'd Rather Walk Than Fly TWA.* We sang, "*We are not afraid, We are not afraid, We are not afraid today, Oh, deep in my heart, I do believe, We shall overcome!*" As I sang that hopeful chorus and other labor songs with all the effort my lungs could muster, I looked around at the battalion of strikers assembled into an angry picket line. Many of them were women with whom I had become close with over the course of my sixteen-year career with the airlines, which had begun in 1970. Now we were all out of work together.

A few months prior, notorious business magnate Carl Icahn had completed his takeover of TWA. This is a man who has since become ingrained in the American psyche as a poster-boy for unchecked corporate greed. First order of business: he promptly got rid of all of the flight attendants and hired a whole new work force. I'll never forget the sense of betrayal and dismay I felt when Icahn did that. I remember wondering, *how am I, and others, going to make it?* I was living in Manhattan, the most expensive borough in the most expensive city in the country. My friends in the industry called me, many of them in tears, all asking the same question. *What are we going to do?* We had no other choice than to stand up for ourselves.

Remember, this was back in 1986 and as I said, the flight attendant workforce was overwhelmingly female. We were, to put it mildly, not afforded a high level of respect by male-dominated sectors of the business world. I don't think the "boys clubs" in the boardrooms expected us to rally and support each other in this struggle for what we believed were our most basic rights. I think most of them, Icahn especially, held onto a sexist image of a 1950s hostess wearing a stylish uniform. How wrong they were! The men running TWA had failed to take into account that our union was strong, and led by amazing women like Pearl Nelson, who would later be a great ally and friend to me after I started SHERPA.

On March 8th our union, the Independent Federation of Flight Attendants, which represented about 6,000 TWA employees, had called for this massive strike. Over ninety-eight percent of the work force walked off the job. This was truly an enormous and difficult undertaking. Together, we put up picket lines at 32 of the 62 domestic airports served by the airline. Through the days and the nights we marched on our picket lines, whether along Fifth Avenue outside their corporate offices or at the TWA hangar and terminal. Picketing all day and night was hard work and of course we weren't getting paid. We sang songs, chanted labor slogans, and did whatever we could to pass long hours in the light of the sun and the dark of the night—and of course in the rain and the snow. The only alternative was to become a "scab," someone who crossed the lines and went back to work. I knew that no matter how horribly bad things got, I would never be a scab. We had to stay strong together.

Back on that picket line at JFK, we all gave one final universal shout: *Flight Attendants Deserve Respect!* And then began to pack up for the day. That was the last day I marched in a picket line. One week later, on May 17, 1986, the strike ended. The union said we had won a "partial victory," but that really wasn't the case. In reality, the airline had been playing dirty. Immediately after the strike began, TWA had quietly hired 2,800 new flight attendants to replace the strikers. Also, as it turned out, some of the existing flight attendants who were let go had in fact crossed the picket lines to return to work. Thinking back, I don't blame those people for going back to work, nor do I think of them as scabs. They were acting out of desperation for their families. The real enemy was Icahn and his insidious business practices in our industry. These practices were deeply rooted in sexism and disrespect for the American worker. It was a decade of greed and corporate raiders.

Icahn wasn't done playing dirty. TWA refused to reinstate more than 2,000 employees who had remained out for the duration of the strike because they said there were no vacancies for them. At age thirty-seven, and for the first time in my adult life, I found myself without a job. I remember being at a loss as to what to do with myself, because I had in fact lost more than just this one job. While serving as a flight attendant, I had taken the time to study, and become proficient in photography and fashion. My airline career also allowed frequent travel to Europe, where for years I had been working as a freelance fashion photographer for high-end brands in the handbag and fashion industry. American and international companies paid me to professionally shop, take photographs, and inform them about the European trends, which were always miles ahead of the U.S.

I photographed Lanvin in Paris, Valentino and Adolfo in Rome, and Milan. Photographing Godiva chocolates in Paris was always a real treat; amazing how everyone loves chocolates, except me. Throughout my entire life fashion, handbags and luggage were of great interest to me. Shopping the market showed me what was happening with fashion trends, colors and style. I was also extremely interested in luggage, handbags, shoulder bags, purses and backpacks, all of which had their own secrets to tell about fashion and function. Little did I know that I was laying the groundwork for something much bigger and more meaningful; that spending so much time in the handbag industry would pay off handsomely in the future when I started my own company. But I still didn't know what I was going to do.

All of my main sources of income, travel and creative passion had just disappeared virtually overnight, since being laid off at TWA meant I could no longer travel affordably, which in turn meant that I lost all of those other overseas jobs as well. A large part of my identity had been stripped away. Very honestly, I was frightened and apprehensive about my future. I didn't know *what* I was going to do. The New York City to Europe life I had spent nearly two decades building had just disintegrated, and I was left in the rubble. How was I going to evolve it into something new and meaningful? What would that "something new" look like?

Today as I look back on this difficult, unemployed, unknowable period of my life, I am able to view it with perspective. I *was* learning valuable lessons about resourcefulness, resilience, and persistence, all of which would serve me well in the future. I certainly was not aware of it at the time, but losing my job with the airline was the first step down a long road that led to me discovering my true calling of founding SHERPA.

A total void had been opened in my professional life. I began looking inward, trying to determine what I really wanted to do with the rest of my life. The idea for the SHERPA Bag, my revolutionary soft-sided pet carrier, would come later. I always knew I would need to do something I loved and helped to make a difference in the world. A solution that filled a void in the marketplace. I thought long and hard. Fortunately, I was able to find my special *raison d'être*. It took the most special little dog to help me find it!

***

1987

I had been working as a professional photographer for many years. Following the loss of my job with TWA, I was hired to work as a portrait photographer at an embarrassing, humiliating $7.25 an hour, which was a very meager stipend to barely keep me afloat over the next year. I was aghast, but I had to keep learning what I had to do to build my talents and professionalism in another format of photography.

I was living with my fiancé in New York City and had always had a deep desire for a dog. I'm sure many other prospective pet owners have experienced this longing. Of course, as a flight attendant I had never been able to have a pet, as the job required too much time away from home. Except for exceptional circumstances, such as the billionaire who once bought out all of the first class section so his two Afghan hounds could travel with him, you couldn't take a dog or cat or any other pet into the passenger cabin with you. I would help change all that in good time, but back then that was simply the way it was.

However, now that I wasn't a flight attendant anymore, I figured it was the perfect time to realize this dream. In September of 1987 my fiancé and I were up in the Berkshires mountains in Western Massachusetts, where we often went for short periods of time to visit with our very good friends and escape the hustle and bustle of New York City. On this trip, I had a feeling that something great was going to happen. It sure did: I met one little puppy who would change everything!

I had heard there was a Lhasa Apso breeder in the Berkshires, so I convinced my fiancé that we should take a detour to have a look. Wouldn't you know it: they only had one puppy left. It was love at first sight. I have a picture of me holding SHERPA for the first time. She was nine weeks old, a tiny thing that would grow into a remarkable companion and business partner. Holding her clutched to my chest I felt warmth in my heart and a loving connection. Every pet is the most adorable creature in the world to its owner, and she was the most adorable to me. From that moment until her last on earth, SHERPA only left my side when it was absolutely necessary. Otherwise, we were inseparable. She became my best friend and gave me the truest unconditional love when I needed it most. She later became my SHERPA brand Ambassador, and the four-footed love of my life.

I'll always remember when I first met SHERPA: September 26, 1987. That day, my life changed in ways that I was not yet able to perceive, but the wheels of change were already in motion. Less than two months later, I would rely on this little bundle of love for more solace than I could ever have imagined. If she hadn't been there on the fateful morning of December 22nd. I don't know what I would have done.

After the Berkshires trip, my fiancé and I returned to our apartment in Manhattan and settled back into our daily routine, albeit with this tiny new addition. From the outset SHERPA was with me everywhere I went, and, as a photographer, I captured it all with photos. Over time, I had successfully trained her to become my perfect little model, an outcome that would prove eminently useful in the future when I began to market my bags, and she would curl up inside and demonstrate how safe and comfortable they were. At the time, I was simply enthralled to be photographing my new best friend.

Soon, however, our tranquility would be shattered. It was the night of December 21. I was having trouble sleeping with a bad cold, tossing and turning, so I went to the guest bedroom so as to not to disturb my fiancé, who was resting peacefully in our bed. After finally dozing off, I overslept and woke up with a start at ten minutes past seven the next morning. My fiancé and I usually left to go into the city at six-thirty a.m., so I was surprised that he had let me sleep. I figured he was dressing, so I jumped out of bed and took a quick shower. My Dear SHERPA sat on the tile in the bathroom as I got myself ready for the day ahead.

Once dressed, I went into our bedroom with SHERPA walking behind me. Surprisingly, he was still asleep under the covers, so I said, "Honey, time to get up. We're late!" There was no response—only an eerie silence. My fiancé was lying motionless, arms crossed over his chest. I tried to shake him awake, but he was stiff as a statue, his skin as cold as marble.

In a state of shock, a huge sinking pit weighing down my stomach, I ran into the hallway of our apartment building and down a flight of stairs to bang on the door of a neighbor with whom I was very close. She opened the door wide-eyed and was immediately alarmed.

"Gayle, what's wrong?"

"Please," I told her. "My fiancé isn't moving. Please call for me. We've got to get help!"

My neighbor called 911, then bolted back up the stairs with me. Of course, my fiancé was in the same motionless position. I couldn't bear to look at his frozen face, the face that just the night before had been talking and laughing with me.

At that point, everything started happening extremely fast. My neighbor took SHERPA into her apartment to care for her while all this was happening. All of a sudden, there were firemen in the apartment. One of them did CPR, and then the word "Clear!" was shouted as they zapped my fiancé's chest with a defibrillator. In what seemed like another instant, I was riding with my fiancé in the back of an ambulance, all lights and sound, thundering down the city streets. I gripped his icy hand

and the side metal bed he was strapped to, both equally cold. Once at the hospital, he was wheeled away from me through the emergency entrance. I sat waiting in a corridor in the hospital, petrified. After a painfully long wait, a nurse walked out and told me he was dead. Surely this was a nightmare I would awaken from any moment. Gradually, through the confusion and trauma of the events, comprehension seeped in. As the emergency room doctor explained, my fiancé had clearly never awakened that morning. He had suffered a massive heart attack and had been dead in bed for many hours. It was as simple and as terrible as that. Though I told myself that, had I been there I could have helped, the medical staff assured me it was instantaneous. There was nothing anyone could have done. At least he did not suffer.

Later, I returned to our apartment, still in a state of shock, one I would remain in for a very long time. When you are in shock, you don't know what you are doing. I was totally in another world. I would just sit there in a catatonic coma like a zombie. I was going through the biggest tragedy of my life to date. My only consolation was SHERPA's unconditional love.

Even though I was in a detached state, to say the least, I still had extremely pressing concerns. I won't get too far into the details, but after my fiancé died I was literally left with nothing. I had just lost my airline job and couldn't afford our apartment, so I would now also not have a place to live. I needed time to process what had happened, and to grieve, but the world was bearing down at me with incredible speed. I was in total shock and grief.

Ten days after my fiancé died, my mother, Connie, arrived in New York. My mother has always been my best friend. Her arrival gave me the first sense of relief I had not had since that horrific loss. I broke down in tears and collapsed into her arms. "Oh sweetie," she said. "Let's get you home to California, at least for now."

We came up with a makeshift plan. I would return with her to her house in Belmont Shore, in Southern California, where I could take some time to grieve and figure out my next steps. My mother wound up buying a car from my next-door neighbor. Since we couldn't fly with SHERPA, our only option was to drive cross-country. Now my mother would be providing me with more of the nurturing and love she had always given me, and SHERPA would continue to be my greatest source of companionship during this nightmare. "Don't worry honey," my mother told me. "We aren't in a hurry anyway. Some time on the road will be good for you."

My mother was a woman of action: She bought a used BMW from the neighbor, and we began our journey from New York to California. As we made preparations, a question popped into my head: How was I going to transport SHERPA in the car so she would be comfortable and safe with all the motion and all the stops and starts? I didn't want to let her roam free on the back seat because that would be dangerous for her. I also didn't want to put her in a hard-sided pet carrier. They did not offer the soft comfortable environment I wanted for her. I looked around the apartment for something she would fit into and managed to find a large enough tote bag. I'll never forget that tote bag. It was a great design for me but not for a dog and didn't work very well. It certainly didn't have the proper ventilation. Regardless, but it would have to do for the moment. I was doing the best I could, putting one foot in front of the other. The continued state of shock and misery were crippling.

"SHERPA looks a little odd in that tote," my mother remarked as we started out. "I know," I said sadly. "It's the best solution I could come up with for now."

For the next ten days we meandered west, driving slowly, not speaking much, even when we stopped for the night at one roadside motel or another. In the car, I would stare out of the window desolately for hours on end. I probably looked like the very definition of "down-and-out." One small source of comfort was watching SHERPA during those long hours on the road. When mother drove, I held SHERPA securely in my lap, the seatbelt holding us both in. She was just watching the day go by. I let her out of the tote bag as often as I could because it wasn't that comfortable for her. I knew there had to be a better way to transport a dog or a cat in a car. We even stopped at several pet stores along the way, searching for a solution. There was nothing available at all. The only pet carriers were the hard-plastic ones with all its limitations, and I preferred the roominess she had in my soft tote bag.

Mile after mile, my mother Connie, SHERPA and I ventured on. I didn't smile once until we reached Denver, Colorado. Clearly wanting to cheer me up, my mother drove us to a Western-themed outpost, which was also called a "Trading Company." There were covered wagons, barrels of hay, and costumes you could dress up in and take a novelty picture. Mother and I donned long settler dresses and cowboy hats, and, holding SHERPA between us, smiled for the camera. It was also the first time I had smiled since my fiancé died.

"You know what's funny," I said, looking at the picture in the car as we continued on the road to California, "Traveling with your pet hasn't really evolved much since the days of covered wagons. The people from that frontier time had the same options available to them as we do today. It's like we're traveling in the Dark Ages when it comes to our pets."

"It's outrageous when you think about it," my mother replied.

"I know I can do something about it," I said, looking at the photo, and then at SHERPA in my tote bag. At that moment, I knew that I wanted to create a product that would make it safer, more comfortable and easier to travel with your dog or cat. I didn't know exactly what that would look like yet, but I felt a sense of purpose. By the time we reached California, I had my heart set on achieving this goal, using all my experiences: my familiarity with airline cabin specifications, including dimensions and configurations of the space in front of each seat, my understanding of high-end handbag design, and my fashion photography.

With three decades of distance, reflecting on this time in my life, I can see how all of these painful events were paving stones that formed the road that led me to create and grow the SHERPA Pet Trading Company and design the first-ever officially approved soft-sided pet carrier that ushered in a revolution in pet travel. Being laid off by TWA injected a sense of urgency into my life. It made me more aware, more willing to take notice. If I hadn't lost my job at TWA, I would also not have gotten little SHERPA, something that seems unbelievable to me now. If my life hadn't been destroyed by the sudden death of my fiancé, I would never have had to start over and never have taken that much-needed road trip, which instilled in me the certainty that things needed to be changed to vastly improve pet travel. In sum, if my life hadn't been destroyed, I would have never had to rebuild it. As I have always said frequently, the best thing about having nothing is that you have nothing to lose. This can be a good thing when you endeavor to rise above your circumstances.

People say that "necessity is the mother of invention." I'm not grateful for the pain and sorrow that occurred in my life by the untimely death of the man I loved. I'm not grateful for having no home, no money and no job during that time. However, I *am* deeply grateful for the lessons all the trials and tribulations afforded me. I am proud that I emerged stronger, more resourceful, with a new purpose to take on the travel world on behalf of all of us who love, cherish and want our four-legged companions with us. The SHERPA Bag was named after my beloved dog of course. With this bag, I created a whole new category: the soft sided pet carrier.

Let me take you back, and show you how my determination, along with that of my devoted mother and my unconditionally loving dog formed a brilliant partnership. You will see what it took to build a major brand that helped change pet travel forever. The good, the bad and the unbelievable continue until this day.

It's in the Bag

Chapter 2

Creating a Category and Building a Business from Nothing

What do you do when you are suddenly left with nothing? How do you pick yourself back up when the ground beneath your feet has shifted and threatens to swallow you up? Each situation is unique in many aspects but also relatable. In my case, I had to turn the pain of losing the man I loved, my job, and my home and somehow turn it into a fire burning inside of me that drove and inspired me to create and build a business! I picked myself up from days of crying in bed and told myself I had no time for this wasted wallowing. I did have angels: my dog, SHERPA, my mother, and my dearest friends. My mother was the best. She was the one that helped me rise above the deplorable state I was in. She rescued me and unconditionally helped me to rise above my sadness and self-pity.

Those were some of my circumstances just before I started the SHERPA Pet Trading Company. It was the end of 1987, and as I said, my situation was with no exaggeration, rather desperate. I had no money, no home and no job, and a grief-filled heart. My despair, depression and fear had put me in a state of shock. Trying to deal with almost more than I could bear, God, my mother and SHERPA stepped in. I was really afraid. I didn't know what to do. I would sit there like I was in a coma. I couldn't think. What in the world was I going to do, when I couldn't do anything?

Deep inside of me, I knew that I must do something significant with the rest of my life. I always tell people that they should create their business around something they love, and I loved SHERPA the dog with all my heart. SHERPA comforted me with unconditional love, always by my side. Our bond of true love was a very special one. Those days of sadness and grief were the beginning of a 17 year long partnership that would go on to become the most important thing I had ever done in my life. It was the birth of a business. A calling that would become a global brand and a revolution in pet travel.

SHERPA's Pet Trading Company began as a one-woman, one dog company headquartered out of a mere six-hundred square foot apartment in New York City. As with all things in life, I had to take it step-by-step, and there were certainly a lot of steps to getting SHERPA Pet Trading Company off the ground. While this time in my life was so very challenging, I just knew I had to do it, and I achieved success. The gratification and pride came to me when I would be on a plane with SHERPA in her bag, underneath the seat in front of me.

I encountered many obstacles to make all this happen. If you want to succeed, you must dream big, have a passion, believe in yourself, work endless hours, focus on your commitment, and take the good with the bad. Believe me, you will find, as I did, that there will be plenty of both. Crying is a waste of time and ruins your makeup. So pick yourself up, do it, and continue to pray with intent.

From its inception till now, SHERPA Pet Trading Company has been the most important part of my life for more than thirty years. I will share with you the story of its trials and tribulations, its growth and its first successes and failures. They are all an important part of what it would one day become. I hope find my story educational, motivational, inspirational, and enjoyable.

The first years of SHERPA's existence as a business were humble, born of sheer grit, and a stalwart belief that this was something I must do. I am sure many people and entrepreneurs can relate to that feeling: you're driven into action with the passionate belief in your business venture as an idea you cannot get out of your head. It is one that grows and multiplies until it becomes a part of the fabric of your being. We are entrepreneurs because we believe, dream and fly above the mess that real life often throws in our path. We see the world with our hearts and souls as well as our minds and senses. And one thing more. I don't have a PhD. I operate from emotional intelligence. We entrepreneurs have no choice. We operate with intent and do the very best we can do. We climb over the negativity. The jealousy and entitlement of people will force us to stand up, be strong and push past whatever is disempowering. You cannot give up. When you find the one thing you really want to do, don't let anything stop you. We are all on our own journey in life. Let me continue to share my very bumpy travels, and hope they inspire.

***

1988

After being with my mother, Connie, in California for a while, I knew I must get back to New York. The TWA strike had ended, and we were called back to work as flight attendants. Our new annual salary was half of what it had been before the strike which came out to $22,500, but when you lose everything, something is better than nothing. I told myself that the flexibility this job offered for travel and the additional income I would make doing fashion photography abroad. Being able to personally and professionally shop trends for U.S. brands that wanted to know Parisian, Italian and other European styles and details, would offset the lowered salary. On some level, I knew I was going back to New York to pursue something much bigger than myself and would be pursuing a new chapter in my life.

SHERPA the dog and I headed back to New York City. Thankfully, I had great friends who let me stay with them while I worked to get back on my feet. Also, when I lost my job, I had to rent out the small apartment I had still kept on 57th Street and 1st Avenue. I included maid service, and I was the maid. The people I rented to were absolutely fabulous. They told me I could stay there whenever they were out of town, which happily turned out to be quite often. New York has a reputation for being a tough city, which always brings to mind the line from the wonderful song, "New York, New York." If you can make it there, you can make it anywhere! During that time when I needed assistance those people, my friends and my apartment renters, were among the kindest, most helpful individuals I had ever encountered.

This period of my life was rough, but in retrospect I can see that it was fundamental in making me the kind of person who is able to rise above, create a business from nothing, and move forward. I knew with every fiber of my being that I must become financially independent, and I never let anyone or any circumstance victimize me and control my life. Even if I had to sleep at friend's houses, and even if I had to work harder for less money, I was totally motivated to never go back to that dark place again. I wanted to be my own boss, and realize my own version of the American Dream. It would take time, but I truly believed I would make it.

First I had to go back to work. Soon enough, I was back at TWA, flying all over, domestically and internationally. While my job solved one problem, not having any immediate income, it presented another one. SHERPA could not travel with me. In 1988, pets weren't allowed in cabin areas, only in the cargo hold areas of planes. Connie would visit me to help take care of my little dog, and friends would also look after her, but I hated to be away from SHERPA for such long stretches. It seemed ridiculous to me that people couldn't travel with their beloved pets. They are such an important part of our lives that to be separated from them is so very disheartening. It got me thinking: Why *couldn't* pets go in cabins with their humans—especially small dogs or cats, like SHERPA? I also wondered why it was so difficult for them to travel with us in other modes of transportation such as trains, buses, and automotive vehicles. These questions rolled around and around in my mind, refusing to leave.

With hindsight, the answer seems obvious, but at the time it was a myriad of puzzling complexities. There was simply no soft-sided, pet carrier bag, in which smaller dogs and cats could fit into, that would allow them to travel safely, securely and comfortably underneath the seat in front of each passenger. Certainly, you couldn't have pets running around freely in the cabin of an airplane, or down the rows of a bus or train. However, you could have a pet on board various modes of transport if the pet was comfortably housed in a lightweight bag that was ventilated and safe and could be intelligently secured in the plane, train, bus or automobile.

Doing my market research, I discovered that there were only hard-sided plastic carriers. While these seemed effective in some circumstances, this was not what I envisioned. These were very serious issues burning in my mind and my heart—as I flew flight after flight for TWA, leaving my beloved SHERPA behind with trusted friends, every time. Then, one afternoon, everything snapped into focus. I'll never forget that day. It was April 14, 1988. I had just returned home from a ten-day work trip and was overjoyed to be reunited with my SHERPA. I loved to stroll around New York with her, so I put her in one of my tote bags and we set off to walk around town. While we were walking down First Avenue and 57th Street, she was right by my side in the tote.

It certainly was far from perfect. But it's all we had at the moment. It was then that I realized that *I* needed to create a *perfect* travel bag for pets! It would be safe, stylish, soft-sided, easy to carry, and, most importantly, wonderfully comfortable for its precious cargo. I would call it the SHERPA Bag! There was obviously no other name for it. SHERPA had been there with me from the beginning, and now we were starting something new, ultimately life-changing together.

I would be remiss if I told you that at that moment I knew with any degree of certainty that I would create a product that would forever change pet travel and other aspects of the human-animal bond. However, I did know I was onto something that must be done. These moments are rare in life, and when such a moment takes hold of you, recognize it and don't let it get away. As I walked through the streets of New York with SHERPA, ideas flooded my mind, and I was filled with passion and commitment.

First things first, before you start any business you must conduct "market research." This is crucial. If it turns out you are thinking of making a product that already exists in the marketplace, you will not be solving a problem for anyone. Why would anyone want to buy your product if there are better options available by established competitors? You must totally research the marketplace, not just domestically but globally.

I set out to do my due diligence, in the process becoming infinitely more knowledgeable with regard to all things related to the pet industry. I pored over catalogues, visited every pet store in the city and all high-end department stores. I even looked at products that various brands were planning to release the next year to see if any of these might already be set to fill the void in the market that I wanted to address.

What I was delighted to find was that nothing existed anywhere like what I was envisioning for the SHERPA Bag, or even came close. I was about to create a new category, for which there was a definite need. While the idea had come completely out of my own need, there *had* to be a better way for everyone to travel safely, comfortably, and stylishly with their pets. Believing I had found the solution filled me with tremendous hope and also a bit of fear. Was I really going to take this idea and start my own business? I knew nothing about starting a business. What if it crashed and burned? Well, you never know until you try...

I was so grateful to be healthy and full of energy, but the defining catalyst that gave me strength was, SHERPA. Since I had already lost everything, I had nothing more to lose. I was still struggling to hopefully get through the worst of this nightmare. Of course, hope is not a strategy and the idea of a soft-sided pet carrier was so important, I committed myself to making the product and the business a reality.

During this time, I had been trying to pick up as many TWA flight assignments as possible that would bring me back to Los Angeles. I loved going back to California to see my mother, who would always be waiting at the gate to pick me up. Soon after my revelation, I had a flight scheduled to LAX. On that flight, I discreetly but meticulously measured the floor space underneath a seat in the passenger cabin. I knew that if I ever wanted to get my bags approved for cabin use they would have to fit comfortably underneath the seat, adhering to airline rules and regulations. I wrote these dimensions in my notebook, adding another element to my vision for the SHERPA Bag. Details and specifications like this will make or break a product when you are building a business.

As I got off the plane that day, there was Connie, waiting for me at the gate as always. This was back before airport security had become as stringent as it is today, and loved ones could greet you immediately as you got off your flight. It was so wonderful she was always there to welcome me home, always impeccably dressed. That day she was dressed head to toe in pink, her favorite color. My mother always had her own distinctive sense of style, and my heart was full when I saw her there.

On the drive from LAX to Belmont Shore, Connie noticed that I was particularly quiet and that I had something on my mind. My mother and I had always been tremendously close, and she could read my emotions. When she began to probe a bit, asking me what I was thinking about, it all came out. I told her about my idea for creating a soft-sided pet carrier that would fit underneath the seat in front of you. I also told her that I had done my market research and discovered that there was a total void in the market place for my idea.

"I just can't get this out of my mind, mother," I said. "I know this is something I *must* do."

"I believe you darling" she said. "I will help you in any way I can."

Those words meant so much to me. I had my first believer in the soft sided SHERPA pet carrier

"I *must* to do this," I repeated.

"The idea is wonderful," she said, and putting on her bookkeeper hat, added: "A business is more than an idea. You have to keep your *financial* house in order. There are day-to-day things you have to keep on top of, when it comes to orders and money, that one person can't simply do alone. What if I managed the finances of the company, and keep the books for you?"

My mother was an excellent bookkeeper, and this was the perfect role for her. I was so overjoyed by her offer. It made everything feel like it was falling into place.

That car ride was the beginning of a long business partnership. I would handle design, marketing, public relations, promotion, and sales. Connie would keep the books and make sure the financials were in order and correct. That benefit alone was a tremendous relief to me. I was so fortunate to have her help in this vital start to building a business since you must be able to fully trust the person who handles your money. There was no one in the world I trusted more than Connie.

Connie also did something else for me before I left California: she gave me five thousand dollars to help start the business. I would have never been able to begin without that investment and her belief in me.

When I returned to New York, it was with the single-minded purpose and commitment of creating the SHERPA soft-sided pet carrier business. First, to supplement my mother's contribution, I went to my credit union and took a modest loan against my flight attendant salary. It wasn't much, but both sums were enough to get me started. Next, I scheduled a meeting with Harold Sachs, who was then president of the Handbag Association. I had worked for Harold for years as a photographer; he had given me assignments all over Europe where I did photo shoots for brands like Valentino, Lanvin and Adolfo. I also was doing photography for Godiva Chocolates. I told Harold my idea and even showed him some sketches I'd been working on. He thought this was a great idea and said he believed in me.

"I *must* do this," I told him when I had finished explaining my vision. "I need an excellent manufacturer to get started."

"You not only need a manufacturer," he replied, "You need a manufacturer that shares your level of attention to detail, and one who will work with your vision and dream."

"The first production of bags has to be perfect," I said. "I cannot compromise on anything. Quality and detail had to be above and beyond."

"There is only one manufacturer that fits your needs," Harold said. "And they are in Korea."

It was 1988, and the doors of trade and commerce with

China had not yet opened, so Korea was the only place where I could have soft-sided pet carriers made to my standards of quality and pricing. I knew that my exact retail price point for the SHERPA Bag needed to be seventy-five dollars, not a penny more or less. That price would allow me to hit my profit margins and build a sustainable business. With the level of quality, complexity and detail required, producing the bag in the United States was totally out of the question.

Harold helped me make the connection with the Korean manufacturer, and within a week I was on a plane to Seoul, specs and sketches on hand. I remained there for ten days, meeting with them and working at their factory outside the city to make sure the bags were being made to my exact specifications.

This was an absolutely crucial moment in the development of the business. Everything depended on the pet carrier being perfect. I showed them my design and went over every detail with them until the sample was perfect. The Original SHERPA Bag needed to be soft-sided, have proper ventilation, be secure, and be large enough for both small and medium size dogs. It needed to have the flexibility to fit under an airplane seat yet be sturdy enough to endure the wear and tear of travel. A shoulder strap was a must, and it had to be lightweight and easy to carry. It also had to be fashionable and stylish. That meant the zippers, straps, stitching and logos all had to be of the highest quality. Everything had to be safe, functional and stylish for airplane travel, and appealing and marketable to customers who shopped at Saks Fifth Avenue, Bloomingdales and other high-end marketplaces. Above all, it had to be comfortable for the pet, with plenty of pockets for their toys, food, water and other necessities. In other words, a little "home away from home."

Happily, I was able to achieve all of these elements to satisfy my vision for the SHERPA Bag, and I left Korea having put in a purchase order for 1,200 original SHERPA Bags, black color size medium. That was the minimum order the factory would allow. Black was the obvious choice for the first bag: if you are dressed fashionably while traveling, black is the number one shade. This original SHERPA Bag design would turn out to be the number-one selling pet travel bag worldwide. But let me not get ahead of myself. I still had a lot more work to do before SHERPA became a global brand and forever changed the way we travel with our pets.

***

1989 - 1990

I incorporated the SHERPA Pet Trading company in 1989, which is why you'll still see "Since 1989" emblazoned on the logos of all of the now extensive line of products. I had designed the original SHERPA Pet Trading logo with the theme of travel in mind. Mount Everest was in the back and SHERPA the dog, along with a generic SHERPA guide, in the forefront. Through the years, I changed the logo to include a cat not a generic SHERPA guide. It was really alarming when I had received a cease and desist from Norbu Norgay, the son of Tenzing Norgay, who was the first Sherpa guide to climb Mount Everest along with Edmund Hillary. I worked with Norbu to let him know that was not his father, or his father's dog in my logo, and sent him a SHERPA Bag for his cat. I had changed my logo and did a press release, to say "the cats would be out of the bag and into the logo with SHERPA", since half of our customers were cats.

In order to prepare for my first order of bags to arrive from Korea, I rented a no-frills warehouse in Queens. To get there, you had to drive over the 59th Street Bridge. It was just about as bare bones a place as you could get, but it was functional and where I had to be. By this time, I had been able to reclaim my apartment on 57th Street, so that became the official SHERPA headquarters. Everything was run out of that little six hundred square foot space. It was very modest, but an exciting start to the business. I lived and worked in my office.

The initial 1,200 bags arrived at a shipping port in New Jersey. I had to time everything perfectly, so I had to know when the shipment was going to leave Korea, how long the trip was going to take, when the shipment was going to arrive in New Jersey—all had to be perfectly planned. Shipping and supply chains were major things for me to learn, and as I worked night and day I was learning. I also kept researching potential clients so I would be able to sell the SHERPA Bags once they arrived. In the retail business, timing deliveries must always be strategically planned because the last thing you want is to create demand and then not enough available inventory to fulfill those sales.

The day the SHERPA Bags were delivered to the warehouse was a very busy day and night for me. I was finally able to see the product I had conceived, designed, manufactured, and shipped, including all of the perfectly labeled SHERPA boxes, the SHERPA logo, product name and item number, country of origin, weight, and numbers of bags in each box. It was exciting!

Once the SHERPA Bags were in the warehouse, I began going store-by-store throughout New York, introducing the SHERPA Bag to buyers. I went to the few high-end pet stores that existed back then, but my main focus was on high-end department stores. I had to get the SHERPA Bag into those markets. Being featured in Saks Fifth Avenue, Bloomingdales and Macys brought the SHERPA Bag into existence in the marketplace.

These luxury department stores all had large, beautiful catalogues they sent out to tens of thousands of customers and potential customers. In the late 1980s and early 1990s, catalogues were what online shopping is today. I needed to get SHERPA Bags into the best catalogues to help the brand expand beyond New York City and quickly reach a national audience.

The first high-end pet store I began with was American Kennels on Lexington Avenue. I walked in with SHERPA, the dog, lying comfortably inside her SHERPA Bag. It felt wonderful to be able to carry *SHERPA* in her SHERPA Bag. Needless to say, SHERPA loved being carried around in her custom-made pet-carrier. She was the first dog in the world to be in one, a four-legged trendsetter.

I went right up to the woman working the sales counter and asked, "Would you be interested in carrying this bag in your store?" She looked at me, looked at the bag, and replied: "Isn't that bag *used*?" To this day, I still get a laugh from her reaction. She had never seen a SHERPA Bag before! "Not *this* one!" I told her. "I am the creator and designer of The SHERPA Bag. I have a shipment coming in and would love to be in your store."

That is how I got my first sale. American Kennels ended up becoming one of my best customers. They have sold thousands of SHERPA Bags there over the years. Soon Canine Styles, the top retail pet store, followed suit, as did others. It was an easy "yes" for pet store customers to buy the bag because there were simply no soft-sided pet travel carriers available in the world, and its safety, comfort and stylish appearance made it popular from the start. I was filling the void in the market.

The first large, fashionable department store I tried was Bloomingdale's. I used the same strategy as I had with the pet stores. I took the bag, with little SHERPA in it, directly to a buyer and began to explain to her. "I can sell a hundred of these just standing here today," I assured her.

"You know why I love this?" she said. "It's because you are the market for your product."

That's exactly what continued to drive the growth of

SHERPA. I was my market. I knew that, like me, people who had dogs and cats loved them dearly and wanted to take them wherever they went. This was not easy to do at the time. I had to do the very best I could do to change that situation. In order to effect change, we need to know our market well with all the variables. I certainly did not know everything and over time kept throwing myself into the fire. I have been burned many times. Thinking back now, I don't know how I did it, working day and night trying to find my way. Primarily, my love for animals drove me, and the people who loved them became my community, my customers, and my cheerleaders.

After working with the Bloomingdales team, I was put into the Bloomindales catalog. As someone who has been in love with fashion all my life, this was a big step in the right direction. More high-end accounts followed after we got our story and ads into catalogs put out by: Saks Fifth Avenue, Macy's, The Ritz Hotel and many others.

Another popular luxury retail company, Hammacher Schlemmer, agreed to feature me in their major catalogue and in their stores. I was opening up and expanding the market for SHERPA. And not only because of SHERPA's quick success in my local New York market. Every buyer I spoke with said the same thing: *There is nothing like this in the market. This product didn't exist before you created it.* That's how I knew I had created something people wanted and needed. The Sherpa Bag filled the void in the marketplace.

This is not to say it was all smiles, handshakes and bliss. It was exhausting! I was working round the clock on my new business while still working as a flight attendant. I was grateful I could take leaves of absence from TWA during the slow winter months of travel. Before I could build SHERPA into a *brand*, I had to make it a well-known, viable *business*. That meant taking care of every aspect of the day-to-day operations. I rarely slept and was totally devoted to doing what I had to do to build a strong foundation for SHERPA.

Sitting at my desk in my small apartment, I designed my own mailers and advertisements. Being a professional photographer, SHERPA was my perfect model. My background in fashion photography allowed me to do all the photos myself, and I made sure every detail in each photo was in total focus. The SHERPA Bag had to be perfectly set up and SHERPA had to be the very best model. This was not an easy task as I did the photography in my small bedroom, where I set up with professional lighting and made sure my little "brand ambassador" was perfectly posed. Her eyes, her tongue and everything with her pose must be perfect. Well, I had a little secret. I would have a small piece of chicken as a little treat for her as we worked together. This gave her a positive association. She wanted that piece of chicken and knew that, if she was a good girl, she would get it. The SHERPA Bag had to look appealing and comfortable for everyone—dogs, cats and the humans who wore or carried them. I spent countless hours making every detail of the pictures perfect.

In those early days, I was my own delivery driver. Whenever I was scheduled to drop off SHERPA Bags, I would rent a U-Haul van for $19.95, drive it over the 59th Street Bridge to my warehouse, with SHERPA riding alongside me, pick up the boxes filled with SHERPA Bags, and drop them off at the loading docks of the major department stores or pet shops. The delivery men were always surprised to see someone like me driving a U-Haul van into the delivery line. The big truck drivers just couldn't believe that there was a woman and a dog waiting in the freight line in a $19.95 U-Haul Van. We patiently waited in line along with all the other delivery trucks.

The first order of 1,200 SHERPA Bags were selling out quickly, so I needed to place a new and larger order. There was a three month "turn around time" until I could have the new bags manufactured with my quality control in place and shipped from Seoul, Korea to the port in New Jersey. Connie and I worked continuously on every detail of what we had to do, to make sure everything was done perfectly. Do you want to know about all the details of manufacturing and shipping? I sure didn't but I had to. If not me, then who would do it? My philosophy is to do the very best that you can do and continue to work with intent. I certainly could have used some relief from those ruff and tuff days and nights, but I had made my commitment and knew what I was meant to do.

I have always had incredible energy, and I really needed it in those first years of building SHERPA Pet Trading Company from the ground up. I was doing everything with my mother and SHERPA, and learning priceless lessons. Knowing how every single detail of each process functioned and evolved was the only and best way to build my business. Later, when I needed to hire people, I would know exactly what was expected of them. Connie handled the financials, inventory, pricing and documentation of the numbers and sales—all in a 39 cent ledger. She was priceless and taught me the financial part, which I had never had an aptitude for. My brain doesn't work that way, which is why we were the best team.

Over the next year, SHERPA continued to grow steadily expanding to other markets in Chicago, Los Angeles and the many cities in the United States where people loved their pets. One of the first major accounts I acquired was Petco, the largest pet retailer in the United States. I flew out to meet with them at their headquarters in San Diego, and was thrilled to hear that they wanted to put in a $22,500 purchase order. That was my annual entire salary as a flight attendant in one single order! I felt as proud as if I had graduated with honors.

This moment of triumph proved to be a hard-learned business lesson. The contract with Petco stipulated ninety-day payment terms. This meant I was guaranteed to be paid three months after I fulfilled the purchase order. Ninety-days came and went. Then ninety-five. Then one hundred. I didn't feel comfortable calling and asking for my money. It felt somehow beneath me since I was brought up to never ask for money. Finally, after radio silence for weeks, I got through to one of their buyers.

"Oh," he said. "We have to return all of your products."

I was shocked and felt like I was going to die. The rug was being pulled out from under me and I was in shock. What was I going to do? Could this be really happening? They promised. How naïve I was. Whenever I get nervous, it always goes right to my stomach. I was speechless.

Soon I discovered that they had never put any of the SHERPA Bags out for sale in their stores, though I still don't know why. How could my bags sell if they weren't on the shelves? They kept insisting that they just wanted to return all the bags. That would have destroyed me: the loss of the shipping costs alone would have been astronomical. Eventually, I was able to work out a plan where I gave them more terms and started advertising the SHERPA Bag in *Dog Fancy* and *Cat Fancy* Magazines. The ads said to call for a store nearest you. I was the operator who answered all calls! Of course, I sent them to the Petco stores. Finally, I was able to speak with Petco's CEO, Brian Devine.

"You can't return the product," I told Mr. Devine. "I will work directly with every one of your stores to sell The SHERPA Bags."

"Really?"

"I will sell every single one of those SHERPA Bags," I said.

Brian Devine agreed, and over the next few weeks I traveled to dozens of stores, making sure that my bags were perfectly displayed and that their sales staffs were educated on the product, so that the customer would know their pets would be safe and comfortable in the bag. If I hadn't done these things, we might have lost our momentum before we could soar, but I did do them, and SHERPA became Petco's number-one selling pet carrier! Needless to say, they paid me for the purchase order and immediately placed another one. In fact, Brian and I still remain in contact, and he invited me to many of his parties, which were always fabulous. He introduced me by saying: "This is the woman who created a category." That makes me very proud, as Petco was the first major superstore that SHERPA was sold in. I was and am very grateful my product was so successful in their stores.

As I look back on the early days of SHERPA, I can see that everything in my life leading up to that point had been paramount in my ability to launch and grow the company. I had been a fashion photographer and a professional shopper so I knew how to spot trends. I'd been an airline hostess and flight attendant, so I knew firsthand how difficult it was to travel with a pet, and the anxiety people felt in doing so without the right carrier. Plus I knew exactly what type and size bags to create to fit underneath the airline seats. I had been comforted by my devoted, loving dog in a time of tragedy, so I knew how important people's pets were to them and how much they wanted to take them everywhere.

I had been through the depths of despair in my personal life, and with the drive and determination those challenges had forged in me the desire I had to succeed, I knew I could turn a dream into a reality. Even though I sometimes joke that I became an entrepreneur *by accident*, my entire existence had been leading me to the creation of this company, for which I am forever grateful.

By the end of 1990, SHERPA Pet Trading Company was successful. We still had many challenges, but this was the #1 officially approved soft-sided pet carrier in the world. I recognized that my greatest challenges, and hopefully some major triumphs, were yet to come. I still needed to get my bags approved by all major airlines, along with numerous travel associations in order to further my mission—giving everyone the ability to take your pet with you wherever you go. This would turn out to be a long and ultimately rewarding process. But the journey, like most of my life, would be filled with highs and lows, victories and setbacks, trials and tribulations. In the next chapter, I'll show you some of the most dramatic examples of those unexpected challenges and milestones.

It's in the Bag

Chapter 3

SHERPA Revolutionizes Air Travel

As I began to fulfill my ambitious vision of building the SHERPA Pet Trading Company into a major brand that people would trust with their precious cargo, every year was an absolute whirlwind. The first year, all the best department and pet stores in New York carried SHERPA Bags. The SHERPA Bags were top-sellers at national pet store chains like Petco, and orders poured in from catalogues. I was always delighted to see people carrying their dogs and cats around Manhattan in their SHERPA Bags.

At trade shows and conferences, people told me that my product had deepened the relationship their customers had with their four-legged companions. I received thousands of letters and heard countless personal stories from people expressing the same message: SHERPA had changed the way people could travel with their pets. From the very beginning, *that* was the real mission of SHERPA.

We all want our pets as part of our families, to be with us as much as possible. You wouldn't leave a son, daughter, husband, wife or other much-loved human behind when you took a trip, so why would you have to leave your pet behind? It gave me such immense satisfaction to know that, because of the work I was doing, travelling with a pet had vastly improved. Through my business, I also built a community of like-minded people—a community that kept building. People told people about SHERPA, and we grew into a connected network of animal lovers that knew what needs to be done here in the United States and around the world, to further help animals and strengthen our bonds with them.

Even as the company grew more visible, there was still much more work to do. A life's worth of work, in fact. I had to constantly keep *working* for what I believed in. Even though the SHERPA Bag had allowed countless numbers of pets to travel safely and fashionably in cars, trains, buses, subways, and other modes of transportation, not to mention being toted around town by hand in the most stylish manner, air travel was still a major obstacle.

In those early days, as I mentioned earlier, I had a SHERPA 800 number that I answered myself. One of the most common issues people called in about was their frustration that they wanted to take their pets with them into the cabin of an airplane and couldn't. They were disappointed by airline policies that forbid bringing pets on-board, even on short domestic flights. Keep in mind that this was in the early 1990s, when there was no such thing as the "emotional support animal" regulations so many people use today, and unfortunately, too often exploit. I'll talk more about this misuse of a well-meaning policy in a later chapter. Believe me, I have a lot to say on that subject!

Still, the only permissible way to take a pet along with you when you traveled by plane, even the tiniest creature, was to put the animal in a hard-plastic carrier in the cargo hold. Even more troubling, harmfully wrong information was circulated that it was a good idea to tranquilize your animal with sedatives before they flew. This was—and still sadly is—an extremely dangerous practice that can be one of the leading causes of animal trauma and even death during travel. Whenever someone tells me they are thinking about tranquilizing an animal before a flight my response is: *Your pet should not be tranquilized,* "Why don't *you* take a tranquilizer!" The combination of drugging an animal and placing it down below in an aircraft is outdated and, in my opinion, has always been unsafe. It was and is not the way people should travel with a member of the family, especially the most vulnerable pets—cats and small and medium size dogs.

These prohibitive, outdated air travel issues were constantly on my mind. The SHERPA Bag was specifically designed to fit under any airline seat, whether in first-class, business class, or coach. From the start SHERPA was never about me. It was about the massive community of animal lovers around the world who wanted to take their VIPs (Very Important Pets) with them wherever they went.

I knew that it was going to take endless effort, outreach, education, and major perseverance if I was going to get the major airlines to change their policies about allowing pets in the cabin. It's important to understand that I was not trying to get a *law* changed: I was trying to change the policies on airlines. This would require me to go to each individual airline, one-by-one, and effectively convince them to approve the SHERPA Bag as a way to transport dogs and cats in airline cabins. I was also determined to work with the automotive industry on pet occupant safety.

The intentions were not motivated by a desire to increase sales. It was genuine concern for animal welfare. I knew there would be no serious issues with the SHERPA Bag, given that I had designed it myself. There was no way I would ever let SHERPA, my devoted companion, travel in anything but the best. That's exactly what I also wanted for every other animal.

Although I began directly working with airlines in 1990, I had been building toward this goal from the moment I started SHERPA Pet Trading Company. If I was going to approach these major companies, I needed great credibility. More than a successful business, I needed to be a recognized and respected member of the animal welfare community. To that end, I partnered with such agencies as the American Society for the Prevention of Cruelty to Animal (ASPCA), the New York Humane Society, the International Air Transportation Association, the Delta Society—which as I noted before is now known as Pet Partners—and many others. I did all the things I had to do in order to establish true credibility. I also attended many industry conferences and gave speeches at an endless round of events and conventions, including one hosted by the International Air Transportation Association in Rome. People began to recognize not only me, but, thankfully, the SHERPA Bag as a uniquely practical, secure, and fashion-favored brand of soft-sided pet carrier.

Working with the New York Humane Society was particularly satisfying for me because they are a fabulous organization. As it so happened, its headquarters was on East 59th Street in New York City, and I was living on East 57th. As I tell people all the time, when you are feeling down go to your local humane society or shelter and be with the animals. Maybe volunteer to walk those shelter dogs. It helps you so much because the animals need help. You will renew yourself while you build positive relationships by helping them. Going over to the New York Humane Society always brightened my day. I always benefited from my time there and would feature many of the abandoned cats and dogs in my photographs and brochures. One time, I used a three-legged cat from their shelter as one of my models for SHERPA product photos. She was a perfect model. I'll always love that cat, and treasure the time I spent at the Humane Society.

Working with Delta Society, which I related was the largest and most prestigious non-profit for qualifying and registering therapy dogs and other therapy animals, was also particularly rewarding. In 1981, when the Delta Foundation was renamed Delta Society the then president Leo K. Bustad, DVM, PhD, was credited with introducing the term "human-animal bond." The organization's motto was: "Touching lives and improving health through the power of therapy animals." I couldn't agree more! Years later, when SHERPA had grown into a much larger company, I donated a great number of SHERPA Bags to Pet Partners. It has always been important to me, and my mission, to give back to organizations that are as deeply devoted to animals and people as I am.

Even as I continued to work at establishing SHERPA's credibility in all areas of the pet world, I also wanted to continue expanding SHERPA worldwide. As a flight attendant, I flew to many European cities, and had already began placing the SHERPA Bag in the best boutique stores in Paris, Rome, Milan, and London. I was absolutely thrilled to see my product in the pet department at Harrods of London. As global expansion was a necessity, I had been purchasing the right to sell in each country around the world. This was a very expensive process that lay the foundation for a global brand. As a lifelong friend of mine told me, it was my reason to be that encompassed everything I did and was clearly what I was meant to do. This could be summed up as, *"If you want, you can."* Those were words I kept repeating to myself, over and over, as I continued my ambitious worldwide expansion.

With the airlines, the challenge was that their policies were always changing: Meeting with an airline company was much different than meeting with a retailer. Though I had been a flight attendant, I did not have any top executive connections in the industry. I could not simply walk into the headquarters of a major airline and ask to speak to a CEO. I had to appeal to those business leaders by going through specific channels, namely writing letter after letter and following up with phone calls.

At first, I would get someone's assistant or secretary. Little by little I began getting through to the right people. There were so many people to talk to, so many departments that had to be consulted to make the changes: policy and procedure managers, In-Flight cargo officers, the head of reservations, people from Health and Safety. Every day, I worked endlessly making calls, opening letters, sending back replies and meeting with people. Connie, who was still faithfully keeping the books, always told me: "Don't say that you work hard. Everybody works hard." Advice like that kept me grounded, even as SHERPA was about to take off into the skies.

It was in the winter of 1992, several years after I had begun approaching the airline companies, that I started to see real results from my efforts. Obviously, large airlines like Delta, Continental, and American were my main targets. If I could get even *one* of these big carriers "on board," so to speak, it would open the floodgates for my cause. I had been able to make some headway with American, having my calls and letters answered in a serious manner. Then, one day, an official-looking letter arrived at the SHERPA headquarters. My hands shook as I broke the seal and began to read. I read the letter again, and again, hardly believing my eyes. The way this story came about was the SHERPA Bag with a Cocker Spaniel was inside the SkyMall magazine on board American airlines. The Cocker Spaniel in the photo was too large to fit inside the SHERPA Bag. I had not finalized the pets on board program with American Airlines yet. Having the SkyMall Magazine inside every seat pocket with the SHERPA Bag and the Cocker Spaniel pretty much expedited the process of getting the policy changed on American Airlines. It still took more time to have every computer and airline personnel updated to the new pet onboard policy. When I finally received this letter, I was in seventh heaven, cloud nine, in complete ecstasy. **I did it!** Yes, one airline at a time...

February 19, 1992

Dear Ms. Martz:

In response to your correspondence concerning your soft sided pet carrier, the SHERPA Bag, American Airlines has examined the bag and found it to be acceptable for use as a carry-on pet container effective immediately.

As you are aware, under seat dimensions vary based on aircraft type, therefore passengers should be advised to check with the airline prior to the day of flight in order to avoid the possibility of any mis-understandings.

Thank you for the sample bag. It was a pleasure assisting you and if I can be of further assistance, please do not hesitate to contact me.

Jeff B. Cantrell

I couldn't contain my excitement. The SHERPA Bag was now the first only soft-sided pet carrier to be approved by a major airline, one that flew 6,800 flights per day to 350 destinations. Reading that letter, a tremendous feeling of energy and purpose surged through my body. SHERPA the dog was standing at my feet. I bent over, gathered her into my arms, looked her right in her adorable little face, and told her: "SHERPA, you can fly!" She wiggled happily. That day was a major victory not only for my vision, but for *all* pet lovers around the world. I was always working on behalf of the animals and their owners, and things were changing for the better.

However, my efforts with American Airlines didn't end with their sending me that wonderful letter of approval. Nothing is ever *that* simple, as we know! I had to continue to work with them to make sure the policy took hold in every aspect of their business. Like any other sizeable business, airlines have lots of departments, staff, and moving parts. If a new policy or procedure is to be truly implemented, each part of the organization has to be educated on it. For example, a Head of In-Flight Cargo could approve my carrier, but if his directive was not made clear to the Reservations and Ticketing Department, my customers calling to book flights for their pet, might be told that pets are not allowed on board. Gate agents also had to be informed of policy changes. The worst thing that could happen would be for one of my customers to be turned away when they tried to board their flight simply because the agents hadn't been properly educated on the policy or did not read the latest bulletins in the computer.

To make sure this would never happen, I worked directly with American to create a list of regulations that applied company-wide. The document was titled: "PETS IN THE CABIN." I made sure it was foolproof, containing all the necessary information in a simple and concise manner so it could be easily understood by employees at every level of the organization. After that was completed, I made sure American sent bulletins and memos to all of its different departments to inform them of the policy change. A policy isn't truly amended unless that change is *implemented*, and I made certain it was. I had no intention of making history only on paper!

Customers also had to be educated with regard to these new policies and regulations. Whenever my 1-800 number rang, I was grateful to be able to share with them the exciting news. My customers were my best sales people; word of mouth traveled globally and SHERPA kept growing. Connie and I also sent out mailers announcing that the SHERPA Bag with their pet inside was now approved for onboard travel on American Airlines. The response was overwhelming. Hundreds upon hundreds of people told me that this was a tremendous joy and relief for them. They could finally take their pet along! A pet is a part of the family.

This was still only the beginning. I needed *every* airline

to join in my pet travel revolution. In April of 1992, America West Airlines approved the SHERPA Bag for use in its cabins. I was delighted that, in their letter of acceptance, they noted that "the carrier is far superior to the standard hard-sided carriers that are traditionally used." That made me smile because I knew it was true. Over the next few years Air Canada, Alaska Airlines, Continental, Northwest, TWA, and United all approved and actively *welcomed* SHERPA Bags on board their airplanes.

It was endless work, as each policy had to be changed individually, one by one by one. I didn't mind a bit, since it was all in service of the greater cause. I even played the part of travel agent by helping my loyal customers choose an appropriate airline, guiding them through policies and how to deal with uninformed reservations and travel agents. There were always issues that needed straightening out because not everyone read the bulletins and thus were up-to-date on the new pet travel policies. All that mattered to me was that pets would fly comfortably with their owners, safe in their SHERPA Bags.

By 1994, I had gotten most of the domestic airlines to approve The SHERPA Bag. I kept receiving many letters and calls from people wanting to fly on Delta Airlines, I knew their policy had to be changed: it was *the* most important to me because Delta Airlines was the largest airline in the United States, running over fifteen thousand flights a day. A lot of pets could be traveling on Delta! I wrote letter after letter, getting no response. Then one day I reached the secretary of the president of Delta Airlines. To my delight, the president of Delta Airlines invited me and SHERPA the dog to meet with them at their headquarters in Atlanta. SHERPA was the first dog to fly on Delta Airlines, first class to boot.

I've always tried to dress my best, and this meeting was the most important to me and to the future of SHERPA. I put little SHERPA in her SHERPA Bag, and proudly carried her through the airport. I boarded the flight, was politely escorted to my seat, and placed SHERPA securely underneath the seat in front of me, overjoyed that this major opportunity was about to happen.

When we landed in Atlanta, I went straight to the Delta headquarters. Waiting there were fifteen of the airline's top executives: vice-presidents, directors of In-Flight Cargo, reservations and operations directors. You name it, they were there. Like everything SHERPA did, she was absolutely perfect. Over the course of the next three and a half hours we worked together on writing new policies regarding pet travel on board all of their aircraft. We discussed everything, from making a reservation to checking in, and boarding a plane. All of the facets of travel had to be addressed with this new component of traveling with a pet. Everyone at Delta was really looking forward to this change, viewing it rightfully as an added service to their customers. It all comes down to service and revenue. When you provide a better service more revenue will come. SHERPA Bags were going to be the first and only soft-sided pet carrier allowed in Delta's cabins.

Like everything that my little four-legged brand ambassador did, she was absolutely perfect. SHERPA the dog was comfortably lying inside her SHERPA Bag at the center of the conference table as we went over every detail of the pet on board policies. After nearly three hours, she stood up, walked out of her bag, looked round at everyone and then went back in, and lay down. The executives stared back, entranced. I held out my hand with an open palm and said, "And that is SHERPA." It couldn't have gone any better if we had rehearsed it. The outcome of that meeting was perfect. I also worked extensively with them on creating the Delta Deluxe Pet Carrier by SHERPA. It insured that anyone who purchased it would never be turned away from a Delta flight with their pet. It was an immediate bestseller and remains popular to this day.

As an aside, I recently took my dog KARTU to our vet in Paris and met a couple there who were transporting their cat in a Delta Deluxe SHERPA Pet Carrier. They told me how stressed they had been about flying with their cat—until they discovered The SHERPA Bag and saw how it solved their problem. It is wonderfully amazing how life can bring you such grateful moments over the years, clearly and literally out of the blue.

What I achieved with Delta filled me with tremendous pride—the sort of pride that can never be taken away. I may not have a masters or doctorate degree, but my work with the airlines along with the education and awareness I was bringing to people, made me feel like I had graduated from a top university with high honors. The proverbial School of Hard Knocks perhaps?

In the end, and I have to keep emphasizing, it was never about me. It's about people and their pets. Every letter I've sent, every battle I've won, every policy I've changed was in service of the bond that we share with our animals. That bond is one of the strongest forces in the world. If I have helped make it a little stronger, it means I am doing what I am meant to do in the world.

It touches me deeply when I hear from people whose lives SHERPA the dog and the company have touched and changed. Over the years, tens of thousands of letters, emails, calls to the 800 number, and social media messages have poured in, and still do. I've even gotten testimonials from such celebrities as Betty White, Liza Minnelli, Tony Bennett and Cindy Adams. The ones from my endearing customers especially mean so much to me. I've included some of my favorite communications below. These are the real heart of SHERPA and the reason I've dedicated my life to this mission.

It's in the Bag

Good day to you, Gayle Martz!

I just wanted to thank you VERY much for your lovely little invention!

It helped me get my sweet, geriatric, 17-year old Russian Blue through a traumatic time of air travel from middle of Arkansas to middle of California! From the second she sniffed it, she loved it! She was sleeping in it within hours!

But I thought that surely after who knows how many hours of travel (at least eight!) and travail in it in airplanes and airports and taxis, what with all those new sights and smells (she's totally stone-deaf) and thousands of strange people, that she'd flee the carrier at first opportunity, never to get with paw's distance from it again, but she STILL loves it!!!!! It's like her little nest; she loves to sleep in it, where it is! *big grin* It says in the instructions that it folds flat for storage, but she'd go nuts if I tried that trick on her, she wouldn't be able to stand not having it somewhere she can sleep in it!

So, thank you from the bottom of my heart for not only inventing this little gem, but for sharing it with everyone else!

Profuse thanks,

Melissa Finley

* * *

Hi!

I'm Summer Richter and I'm a 6 month old Yorkie Girl. What am I doing? I'm sitting in my SHERPA Bag ready to fly with my Mom from Chicago to Tampa, Florida. The noise of the airport scared me pretty badly, so I kept snuggled up nice and quiet all through the trip. Thank you Sherpa for making me feel right at home!

Summer And Christina M. Richter

* * *

Dear Ms. Martz:

We are leaving Tuesday for Florida, and I just want to take a minute to thank you from the bottom of my heart for your commitment to helping pets (and their people) travel a little easier. We use to drive to Florida every year (we live in Maine) because we figured our Chihuahua would have to be stuck out in the back of the plane. She would be devastated. But last summer, we asked the airline if there was any way possible for our baby girl to be with us on a flight. We explained that we would not fly if she could not be with us, And we were told that if we got an airline approved soft kennel, we would be allowed to have her with us (for a fee of $100.00 round trip). I went looking and that's when I found the SHERPA Bag. She was totally relaxed and slept for most of the trip. I start about a month before we go on a trip, putting her in her SHERPA Bag for a few minutes every day, doing house work, or walking around outside, getting the mail, whatever, so that she is all set to spend several hours in there flying and moving around the airports. That little bag that can hang off my shoulder like a pocketbook has just made travelling so much easier for us that I had to e-mail you and say thanks.

-Susan Chevalier and Tequila

As you can see, what I achieved in pet travel touched people in real and deep ways. I have thousands more letters like these, and treasure each and every one. Traveling with a pet can be difficult, and I'm glad I've helped alleviate some of the challenges involved. On that note, from the very beginning I had written two columns. One called "Travel Tips" from my perspective and another, "Travel Tails" from SHERPA the dog's perspective. These were educational tools that helped spread information and hopefully helpful strategies and practical advice for traveling with your pets.

The suggestions apply equally to travel by car, train and bus. SHERPA is so much more than just a bag for traveling onboard an airplane. I worked with the automotive industry in Detroit on pet occupant safety. This was so important because no one had ever dealt with pet occupant safety. One day, I received a call from the Lear Corporation, an OEM, (an original equipment manufacturing company that make a part used in another company's product). This was really a very big time for me as the whole automotive industry needed to be addressed on pet occupant safety in cars. A dog that is not seat belted inside a SHERPA Bag or safely seat belted into the car, is very dangerous. With all the accidents that happen, slamming on the brakes, the dog or cat becomes a projectile crashing into the windshield, which is very, very dangerous and life threatening.

Having pets in the car can lead to distracted driving, which is a leading cause of motor vehicle accidents in the U.S. According to the NHTSA (National Highway Safety Administration), 8.5% of injury fatal crashes in 2019 were a result of distracted driving. With almost 30% of pet owners admitting that their pets in the car causes a distraction (AAA Pet Passenger Safety Survey, 2011), it's clear that strapping up your dog is an essential part of car safety. According to the AAA Pet Passenger Safety Study, nearly 56% of Americans transport their dog in their car at least once a month. Traveling with pets can be fun, but remember to always be safe when you take a road trip with your furry friend.

I want to end this chapter by providing you with a list of "Travel Tips" you can refer to when traveling with your pet. These are not limited to air travel, although that form of travel is covered extensively. Because pet travel is a dynamic industry, constantly in flux, the most current list of these tips can always be found at my website: www.gaylemartz.com. Happy travels!

Travel Tips:

Train and Familiarize Your Pet with the SHERPA Bag

Before your trip, leave the bag open with a favorite toy or treat inside. Allow your pet to wander in and out of the bag, praising and rewarding it for doing so. Carry your pet around in the bag so it becomes comfortable in this new environment, and will associate the SHERPA Bag with a pleasant experience. The more comfortable your pet becomes with the bag at home, the less anxiety you will have when you travel. The bag will become your pet's private den, a safe space for them to take refuge in. Patience is key. Also, please never leave your pet alone in a zipped-up bag.

Plan Ahead

When you make your airline reservation, be sure to make one for your pet at the same time. Do this as early as possible. Only a limited number of pets can be transported on each flight. That number is low, and varies by airline and aircraft type. Airlines also charge a fee for your pet to travel in the passenger compartment. Those fees vary.

Airline Restrictions

When you make reservations, ask if there are special restrictions for pets in the passenger compartment. Rules, regulations and changes might vary from airline to airline, so be sure to check first. Dimensions for pet carriers are for hard carriers and do not apply to SHERPA Bags, since it is an airline-approved pet carrier that is soft-sided and flexible. The important thing is the size of your animal. Pets must be able to fit comfortably beneath the seat in front of you and have room to stand up and turn around in the bag. Incidentally, don't you wish you could do that in your airline seat?

Absorbent Liners

Airlines insist on these. SHERPA Bags have liners, and you can also add a towel. Take extra towels in case your pet gets motion sickness. Disposable pads are also helpful. Always keep a clean liner in the SHERPA Bag. Easily washable liners make the trip more comfortable.

Health Certificate

There is a zippered pocket in your SHERPA Bag designed to hold a recent (within 7 – 10 days) health certificate from your veterinarian. The statement must include current inoculations. It is essential to have this certificate when flying or when entering some states in an automobile. Be prepared!

Provisions

I always carry an accessory pouch attached to my SHERPA Bag or in my carry-on luggage. The pouch ideally contains your pet's current favorite toy, grooming supplies, plastic waste bags, a few wee-wee pads, a leak-proof (empty) water bottle, and a small amount of dry food and treats. The water and food will be needed after your pet gets off the airplane. We all know liquid cannot be carried through security so make sure to plan ahead. The supplies will also be handy when traveling by car.

Feeding

Feed your pet lightly when traveling. To prevent airsickness, no food should be offered within six hours of departure, and no water within two hours of flight time. An ice cube in a little sturdy water-filled dish will provide refreshment and entertainment during the trip.

Walk Your Fellow Traveler

Before you enter the terminal, take your dog for a stroll away from the entrance and other travelers. One of those plastic bags in your accessory pouch will come in handy for pick-up and proper disposal of your dog's waste. If you forgot or packed away a leash, use the strap from your SHERPA Bag.

Keep Your Pet in the Bag

Your pet should not be let out of the pet carrier from the time you enter the terminal until you reach your destination and exit the terminal. This is a training issue and is also in your pet's best interest. Inserting your hand in the bag and stroking your pet during the flight will be soothing, but make sure the leash is attached to the safety ring inside the bag. Watch the zippers. Keep them both pulled to one side to keep your pet from sneaking out.

Keep a Low Profile

Being on board an aircraft with your pet is a privilege. Surprisingly, there *are* passengers who do not like pets. The SHERPA Bag is designed so as to not call attention to the fact you are carrying an animal. We've worked hard for this privilege, so let's be considerate and not attract any unnecessary attention.

Safety is Our Bag

Practice safety. Always make sure your pet has an identification tag on its collar, and use the leash ring. Practice safety in the automobile too. Place the SHERPA Bag in the middle of the back seat length-wise. Hook the seatbelt through the strap and tighten it. If the SHERPA Bag is on the end of the seat put the shoulder belt through the strap.

In this chapter I told you how I built a global brand and how I did it on a shoestring. To those of you who want to build a successful business, I offer the following advice. The key to you doing this successfully will always be to have a vision, a dream and a goal. Commit yourself to doing the very best that you can. Of course, you need to work very hard, although, again, my mother admonished me to not complain because, according to her, *everyone* works very hard. Identify a void in the market-place that interests you, ideally something you want or need that you perceive as missing. Carefully do your due diligence and research to see if others have that same need. Make sure no one else is doing it. When I saw that other animal lovers had the same unmet need as I did, the light bulb went off and SHERPA was born. It is as simple and as profoundly important and exciting as that.

Now, let's see what success looked like in the days ahead, at a time when it seemed like all my efforts had paid off and nothing could possibly go wrong!

https://petcentral.chewy.com/keeping-dog-safe-car
https://www.wikihow.com/Travel-by-Car-with-Your-Dog

Chapter 4

Increase Visibility, Awards, Buy-Out Offers

As SHERPA, the first officially approved soft sided pet carrier, began to rise to the top of the pet industry, people asked me: "How did you come up with such a great idea?" I didn't think that they were asking the right question. Yes, an idea is important, but in itself means nothing. It's all about what comes after the idea. You must establish the strongest foundation, as the endless amounts of difficulties, logistics and matters will arise. You must continue doing market research regularly, especially when you're first in a category as I was, because when you are successful an overabundance of copycats can and undoubtedly will arise. I certainly have had more than my share. You have to do a million different things you never even thought about before you endeavor to start a company. In truth, you don't always know what you are doing until you try. I was not a Harvard graduate but I did know that I had to do whatever I could to make my dream come true for people and their pets.

In Chapter Two, I told you the story of how I came back from the brink of tragedy and built a business from nothing. In this chapter, I'm going to take you on a journey that will show you *how* I built SHERPA into a global brand, and how devoting your life to a singular purpose evolves, impacts and changes you. This is my story, yes, but most of all it is a story I hope you can relate to, be inspired, and motivated from, especially if you are thinking about going into the business world. No matter what stage you are in, you have to believe in yourself and reaffirm this belief each and every day as you strive toward your goals.

When I ventured into the business world, I entered a new universe. With everything I did there was always a new challenge. I continue to learn to this day, not only from what I did right, but even more from all the mistakes I made. The continuous challenges I experienced over the twelve-year period, from 1990 to 2002, were both difficult *and* rewarding. The most beneficial experiences were those that helped me to know what I was capable of.

They are the products of decades of personal growth as I discovered daily what I was doing and was meant to do. The age old proverb, "If at first you don't succeed, try, try again" may seem clichéd, but it's okay if need be, "Fake it till you make it." The goal is to never let anyone know how out of your depth you may be feeling at times.

Here are some lessons I'd love to share with you:

1. **There must be a driving force that you believe in at the heart of your business.** By now you may be familiar with my philosophy that everyone has a purpose on this earth, and that once you find yours, you must let it color and motivate you in everything you do. That way, when the going gets rough, you, the tough, get going. You must also be motivated by something greater than the possibility of financial gain.

2. **Be resilient and constantly rise above.** Hard times are a reality in life and business. Nobody knows this better than I do, after finding my fiancé dead in bed. Surrounding yourself with trustworthy, caring people will help you to handle the damage and depression that tough times can bring. The fact that my mother always kept our financial house in order, starting with a thirty-nine cent general

ledger, and moving to hundred thousand dollar accounts, was what gave me the strength in the toughest of times. Connie was my biggest support, business partner and best friend. In order to build a business your financial house must be in order. (Employees are discussed in another chapter, so stay tuned.)

3. **Experience the moment.** There is nothing quite like the feeling of being on top of your industry. If you climb that mountain, breathe in the air and enjoy it. At the same time, make sure you are taking time for yourself amid all of the inevitable day-to-day pandemonium. This is something that I certainly never did over the years. Running a business will take over most of your life, but you need to keep *some* part of yourself secret, sacred, and just for you. And practice enlightened self-care: eat right, stay active, and sleep tight.

4. **Remember that your strengths and weaknesses are the strengths and weaknesses of the company.** Get the support, advice and leadership you need from people who know things you don't. Surround yourself with good, trustworthy people.

5. **Go to the places you love, and always bring your pet along on the trip, even if it is just to the park, the beach or a bench under a tree. Their unconditional love, caring, support and pure joy will add so much to your life.** I'll never stop saying this to everyone I meet!

***

1990 - 1995

As I previously described, once I had gotten the SHERPA Bag into all the top department stores in New York, my first major pet store account was the big superstore Petco. After I persevered through my problems with them, the SHERPA Bag became a top-seller in all the Petco stores. The other major retailer was PetSmart, and I was totally elated to acquire their business in 1993. As always, I worked directly to educate their employees about the merchandise so they could effectively point out its superior features and functions.

It's important to understand that even though the SHERPA Bags had started to sell in large numbers, my business was still largely a one-woman operation run out of my six hundred square foot apartment on East 57th Street. At that time, I wore many different hats: I designed new bags, distributed and shipped the bags, and answered my own 800 number. Through it all, I also traveled constantly, to pet shows, gift shows, and premium and incentive shows to market and sell my product in different stores. I also travelled to the PetSmart headquarters in Arizona, to the Petco offices in San Diego, and all around the country to meet with airline representatives in order to get more pet travel policies changed. By 1994, I had succeeded in getting the SHERPA Bag approved on ten major airlines and carried in hundreds of stores across the country.

One of the strategies I was the most proud of was all the successful work of SHERPA the dog did as the company ambassador and "spokes dog" She was the top dog and positively influenced people and the marketplace. My creative ideas were endless and, having always had a passion for design, photography, and writing, I put these skills to use in creating outreach materials for my brand. I created my own catalogues, using SHERPA the dog as my model, and sent them out to veterinarians, breeders, groomers, pet Stores and who ever I could think of.

Catalogues, as important as they were, were also just the tip of the iceberg in terms of my marketing strategies. I created mailers such the SHERPA "Ticket-To-Travel," which was designed to look like a ticket to bring a pet on board a plane. It functioned as an educational tool to let people know that, with the SHERPA Bag, traveling with their pets was now a possibility. Around the holidays, I sent out a Christmas mailer with the tagline: *"SANTA TRAVELS FIRST CLASS WITH SHERPA!"* so people would know they could bring their pets with them when they went home for the holidays.

Additionally, I attached to each bag and sent out an informative "Passport to Travel" filled with travel tips for people and their pets. I also created the "SHERPA and Friends, SHERPA Minis," which were adorable plush pet dolls. These promotional items came with a free mini travel bag and a brass I.D. pendant for the cuddly little travel companion. In addition to being a great way to increase sales, these marketing techniques served a second purpose: to turn SHERPA the dog into an instantly recognizable mascot for the brand, so that people would look at her image and her name and instantly think *pet travel!*

Earlier, I also described my "Travel Tails by SHERPA." This was intended to educate people about travel Petiquette, a term I invented. Written in SHERPA's voice, it implored people to *stop treating their pets like luggage!* It was such a joy to be able to write from the perspective of my best friend and travel companion. I'll give you an example of one of my favorites:

This tale begins along the California coastline on a sunny winter day. A plane flies overhead, reminding me that my flight back to New York with Gayle is only hours away. I'm not at all nervous, as I know I'm safe in my SHERPA Bag, my reservation has been made, all of my important documents for travel have been taken care of and everything is packed and ready to go. With all the things I simply cannot live without, traveling and seeing the world with your best friend is a wonderful experience and needn't be too stressful. Just remind your two legged companions to think ahead and always be prepared. A human should be able to handle that...

The "Travel Tails" series was a huge hit with my customers. They were accompanied by "Travel Tips" written in my voice, more straightforward advice-based pieces, designed specifically to educate travelers. In addition to being attached to every Sherpa Bag, Connie and I were mailing them out widely to increase awareness and education, I also sent them to newspapers and magazines. As SHERPA the dog continued to grow into an increasingly recognizable figure, the press began to take notice. I was grateful and overjoyed to be able to have articles about the little brand ambassador, and the business, in *The Wall Street Journal, The New York Post, The Fresno Bee, Woman Wise Magazine, and The Weekend Journal,* among many others. The response to all of this coverage was always the same: people were delighted to learn that they could travel with their pets!

I'll never forget the first time *The New York Post* ran a story about us. The headline was "Ex Stewardess finds million dollars in doggy bag." You have to understand just how popular *The New York Post* was in the 90s: there was a newsstand selling it outside everyone's building. To be featured like that was a major accomplishment for me. Virtually overnight SHERPA became the talk of the town. Everyone in my building had already read the headline and I was ecstatic when I picked up that issue at the news stand downstairs. I was so proud and happy that I confessed to buying every copy they had to give out.

The day the article came out, the first of several times we would be featured in *The Post,* and my 800 number began ringing off the hook. People were calling in from all over the country wanting more information about SHERPA. At the time, I had no one working with me. As time went on, I had one "helper," a wonderful friend of mine named Mark who was a phenomenal pianist. We had met at the gym, and he had a passion for animals. Mark helped me answer the phone calls as they came in. As the volume of calls continued to increase it soon became clear that I was going to need more help. SHERPA was also now outgrowing my humble apartment. A special credit goes to my doorman, Jose, who always helped me with my heavy boxes, and never told the management that I was running a business out of my apartment, which according to my lease was a "no-no."

For many reasons it was high time to stop living in my office. I decided to rent an office close by in one of the most fabulous older buildings that one of my close friends owned. It was on East 55th Street and Lexington Avenue, which meant I only had a couple of blocks to walk to work with SHERPA. Oh excuse me, she never walked as she was always comfortably carried by me in her SHERPA Bag. Given the steady growth of the company, it was necessary to hire the first employees of what would eventually become a staff of fourteen. Together we became a well-oiled machine. For the first time, I was able to delegate some of the work. This allowed me more time for public appearances, and radio and television interviews. I realized I could turn the SHERPA Pet Trading Company into something larger than the sum of its parts. My horizons expanded. Soon we were able to take over a second floor of the townhouse, and then a third. It seemed like the phones never stopped ringing. SHERPA the dog was continuously featured in dozens of news articles as awareness of pet travel continued to grow, and the company was also growing dramatically.

In a single year, we sold over 28,000 SHERPA Bags and had sales of over 1.5 million dollars. Not bad, considering that only a few years before I had delivered initial orders myself in a $19.95 U-Haul truck rental. I also upgraded my own living quarters and work space to a penthouse in my 57th Street building. For the growth of SHERPA, it was absolutely necessary to constantly update and preview new photo images of new products, I loved the opportunity to have a photo studio set up in my home office. I can't say enough about the benefits that came to me from having the penthouse in my building. There was no one else on the floor, and the view from the penthouse was something out of a dream: all of Manhattan lay before me like a shimmering paradise. When I watched the sun set over the city, I felt as though I had found my place in the world. I was doing what I had been put here to do, and succeeding at it. After all the hard work and struggles, yet I knew that my work was far from finished, even though moving on. You will always be pulled in a thousand different directions. Therefore it is vital to make time to appreciate your life on a personal level. Otherwise, the endless obligations and concerns can cause you to lose sight of who you truly are. As I said before, even when the world around you seems to be moving at warp speed, you must always take care of yourself, or the stress that comes with a business can kill you. I belonged to a gym, and called the Stairmaster "The Sweatmaster" because it was a necessary workout. I also started yoga, which helped me in every phase of my life. Mind, body, spirit is what yoga is all about, and truly the reason I was able to work as much as I could.

***

1996

One afternoon, just as I was photographing SHERPA the dog for an upcoming catalogue, since we were launching a new luxury bag called "The SHERPA Roll-Up," my phone rang. To my surprise and delight it was a representative of The Small Business Association, informing me that I had been selected to receive an award as "A Woman of Enterprise." This award, which was sponsored by Avon, was going to be given to me before a large audience at an event being held at the Waldorf Astoria Hotel.

I was shocked and thrilled. This was not the first award I had ever received, but it was particularly significant. Six years earlier, in 1990, I had worked at this very same event as a photographer. That job came during the very early days of SHERPA, at a time when I really needed the money. Doing their photography that night turned out to be a major step to help me in the growth of SHERPA. Besides the spectacular event being glamorous, I also was able to talk with all of the incredible women who were being honored. When you are taking portrait photographs it is important to get to know your subject and get them to open up to you. It makes the photos warmer, more candid.

As I photographed each woman, she would tell me her story about how she had overcome her obstacles, including some horrific things, and had risen to become a successful "Woman of Enterprise." At the time, I was trying to start something, and to do something new with my life. Those conversations were pivotal moments. I remember saying to myself: "I can't let my problems stand in the way of my purpose." I was truly motivated by these women.

I believe many of my readers may well be in the same situation I was back then. You have an idea, can see yourself doing something with the idea, but don't quite know how to begin. I'll tell you what I realized that day: when you say you are going to do something you cannot allow fear to stop you. You must try. The worst thing that can happen when you try is that you fail. And if so, so what! Failure is only a lesson in how not to do something. You can always keep trying until you succeed!

Six years after that epiphany, there I was, sitting in my penthouse on East 57th street, overcome with gratitude. I had gone from photographing the event to becoming a guest of honor. There was only one problem: I had to give an acceptance speech. I had spoken in public many times before, but this was entirely different. I was going to be in front of the very best women from different industries and several other business arenas, along with dozens of reporters, and television cameras. I must have gone over my speech a thousand times, but I was still convinced that I was going to trip as I walked up to the podium, or flub and forget my words. I had no choice—I had to push through the fear. This event had the potential to be a total launch for me and for the SHERPA brand.

Looking back, this was the moment that I, as an individual, was going to step into the spotlight and become the face of everything I had been fighting for over the last decade. Up until that point, everything surrounding the company had been carefully branded with SHERPA the dog as the ambassador. Now it was *my* turn to position myself as not just the creator of the line of SHERPA Bags but as a thought leader in my industry. I had to push through yet another layer of fear in order to reach a new pinnacle of success. My mother was so proud, and came in from California to be with me.

The night of the awards, I put on a stunning tangerine dress with matching blazer, clasped a pearl necklace around my neck, gave myself some last words of encouragement in the mirror, and headed to the Waldorf Astoria on East 50th Street. The event was even more posh and glamorous than I remembered, and now I was among those being photographed. I shook hand after hand, smiling even though I was terrified.

This was another instance where my training as a flight attendant helped me in the business world. Even if there is terrible turbulence or some other kind of an emergency during a flight, the cabin crew must maintain poise and not show fear. I had actually spent hours at home and in front of my office staff, practicing my speech. That night at the Waldorf, I told myself, "It's just turbulence. You can handle it" as I took my seat in the front row in a room filled with 1,500 powerful people.

After they ran a short video that showed the story of SHERPA's beginnings, the host called my name. I stood up and carefully made my way up to the podium. I could see television cameras rolling and the bright lights of flash bulbs bursting. I gathered my resolve and began to speak. "I had really hoped to have SHERPA speak to you today, but she got scared and decided to stay in her bag," I said with a broad smile. The line got a huge laugh. I paused for a moment, letting the positive energy of the laughter seep over me. *I can do this*, I thought. *I will do this!*

"I can't say that I blame her," I continued. "Speaking in front of such a distinguished and accomplished group would frighten anyone. I still recall how moved I was six years ago when I was given the opportunity to photograph these awards. To learn what the honored Women of Enterprise had overcome and achieved that evening was truly inspiring. My dog SHERPA has inspired me too. With her and an idea, I went from a time where I felt as if I had nothing to this podium today."

As I said those words, I felt their significance ripple through my soul. Here I was in New York City, with cameras filming my every move and thousands of eyes fixed upon me, all because of this incredible journey SHERPA the dog and I had started together. I was grateful to be here, and was starting to feel comfortable in the spotlight.

"I made my dream come true by doing the best I could every day," I told the crowd. "I am deeply honored to have this recognition from Avon and The Small Business Administration. From photographer to recipient, I hope I am one more example of what you can do when you make a commitment, work very hard, and believe in yourself. SHERPA and I thank you!"

As I stepped down from the stage to warm and enthusiastic applause, I knew that my life had changed in some definable way. It was not only the exterior validation that I had received: something inside had changed as well.   That inner strength, the further belief in myself, helped me navigate the media attention that followed. Since there were so many reporters in the audience that night there was even more interest in not only the story of SHERPA Pet Trading, but also my personal story. Suddenly, I was on CNN talking about very personal issues. I also filmed a ten-minute segment on "The Big Idea" with Donny Deutsch, which at the time was a massively popular program. I was featured on NBC's "The Today Show" and on Fox News. NBC also sent a reporter from their show, "Real Life," to come to my home to film an extended segment, where I talked about losing everything and building my life back up from nothing.

Over the next few years I was interviewed so many times that I lost count on television programs, and radio shows, and featured in magazines and newspapers. I have all these interviews saved in my current office, and am always inspired. I was telling my story so I can hopefully inspire others, especially women, as other accomplished women continue to inspire me. Every media interview I did, whether it was with a magazine, a newspaper, or on television, was with the intent to build credibility, sales, education, and awareness of pet travel. The thrill of seeing myself on television or in the paper never diminished, and the impact was noteworthy. My gratitude came from knowing that I *was* making a difference for pets and the people who love them unconditionally as I do.

***

1997 - 2002

Shortly after my speech at the Women of Enterprise Awards, I was contacted by a company offering to buy SHERPA Pet Trading Company from me. Several other companies had also wanted to buy the SHERPA brand. The price tag this company offered was four and a half million dollars. Remember, this was 1997, so four and a half million dollars adjusted for inflation in today's market, is just over seven million. That would have been enough money for me to live comfortably for the rest of my life, with every luxury for my dogs. It would have been the fulfillment of any financial goal I could have possibly dreamed up for myself.

Without hesitation, I turned them down. Why? Why *would* I, a woman who in the not-too-distant past had been left with nothing, reject the comfort and stability afforded by that sum of money? I will tell you why, and I hope it makes sense to you. It was because I felt I was not yet at the end of my journey, but instead at the beginning of a new phase of it. In terms of the business, SHERPA was a global brand, wielding the kind of influence enjoyed by brands like Gucci or Chanel. I knew the company would continue to grow under my guidance, and could not see myself relinquishing that kind of control. Certainly not yet!

There was more to my reasoning. Perhaps even more significantly, I felt like I was on the cusp of a new awareness that I, as a public figure, could bring to my mission as a brand ambassador for pet travel. I wanted to help the whole world do what they loved in the places they loved with the pets and people they loved. Now, with the heightened visibility brought on by this prestigious award, I was in a better position to deliver this message to the world-at-large. I had, in some sense, summated the mountain of success. Now it was time to use that platform to further educate people on what could and should be possible in terms of pet travel—and, along with that, the human-animal companion bond itself.

Over time, as my journey to accomplish these goals continued, I also attracted the attention of celebrities. It was something that I dreamed of only a few years before. Imagine my delight when I opened up *Travel & Leisure Magazine* to read an article in which marvelous Tony Bennett raved about how happy he was now that his Maltese, Boo, could accompany him almost everywhere in his soft-sided SHERPA carrier. In 1997, dog lover and beloved comedian Joan Rivers praised me and the benefits of the bag in her memoir, *Bouncing Back: I've Survived Everything… and I Mean Everything… and You Can Too!* I certainly had survived a lot, though maybe not as much as Joan Rivers had, may she rest in peace. It was fun and flattering to rub shoulders with famous people, and really I appreciated the attention they brought to my mission. It was heartwarming to see how "real" even the most iconic or seemingly remote celebrity or other VIP became in the presence of their four legged friend—or when they met my SHERPA or other tiny "business executive."

With all this, it might seem to you at this juncture that my life and business were now rose-colored, that I was all set, with smooth sailing ahead. Sadly, this was not the case. That kind of resolve would be necessary to handle what was coming next. In the next chapter, let me take you deep under the company to show you how it functioned, and what I had to do to help SHERPA become and remain a top global brand. After that, I will show you how other people's greed, jealousy and betrayal would threaten the very foundation of my company, testing me in ways I could never have imagined, not even on my worst days. Turn the page, and if you like, watch my face: see how I handled the sudden and unexpected turbulence ahead. Smooth sailing is wonderful, but challenging times show us what we are *truly* made of.

***

Chapter 5

Hard-Won Lessons from My Life's Mission

SHERPA guides take people to the top of Mount Everest, the highest mountain in the world. They are charged with making their trek safe, fun, and rewarding. SHERPA, the company, was also based on traveling safely and enjoyably. When you are successful, there are always people who will be trying to take your place faster than you can imagine, and you have to find ways to stay on top. Your company will only succeed if you keep a laser focus on every detail that must be totally defined: a focus driven by the mission that impelled you to start your venture.

I have given this chapter a structure that I hope will prove useful to you in terms of how to run a business that is in line with your purpose. I am going to offer you stories about the period of SHERPA's history that ran from 1993 to 2007. These will provide you with an insider's perspective of my experience and insights into what the business world was like back then. At the end of each story, I will explain how the lessons learned can be applied to help you. The technology, distribution channels, and market trends may have changed with the times, as is inevitable. Still, I believe that the core concepts and insights I describe all remain the same.

My hope is that these stories will inspire you to be the best at working in your corner of the global marketplace. We each have something unique inside of us we want to share with the world and don't always know how. So let's begin by rewinding back to 1990. That was when I started a photography contest intended to deepen my connection with the widespread community of pet lovers around the world that traveled or wanted to travel with their pet.

One of the biggest joys in my life was and still is seeing my four-legged customers quietly and happily traveling in their SHERPA Bags. One day when I was photographing SHERPA, the dog, who was always my best model, I had an ingenious idea. Knowing that many others would want to photograph their pets the way I did, and further, would want to share those photos with the world if they could, I created "SHERPA'S Annual Pet Photo Contest." I had people send in photos of their beloved and adorable pets in a SHERPA Bag traveling around town or somewhere in the world. They had to be in a SHERPA Bag in order to win a prize. The winners would be featured on the SHERPA website and in the SHERPA newsletter. Of course, these fabulous contestants would receive a SHERPA product. Since I was the judge, everyone won.

This was a never-ending contest. I set it up so that we would get continuous photos and endearing letters, usually "written" by the pet. Those were the best. Everyone had a story to tell. This, along with an award-winning photo of their pet in a SHERPA Bag, naming it the "Annual SHERPA Pet Photo Contest," gave it a little extra incentive to get people involved with the pet-loving community of cats and dogs. I continuously received photos and stories from all over the world! The best thing about this contest was that it created a community of like-minded people and gave them a way to communicate with me, to help with our revolution in pet travel.

They were all wonderful and inspired me to do more. My heart was full of joy to see all the photos of dogs and cats. We continued to build our community worldwide. I loved seeing the creativity, ingenuity, and dedication people had in communicating their love of their pets and being able to travel with them.

Here is an example of one of the many great entries I received over the years.

Lorraine sent a photo and wrote:

This is a photo of my 3 ½-year-old Cairn Terrier, Abbey. The picture was taken in the San Jose, California airport on the way home to Chicago/O'Hare. She really enjoys her SHERPA-on-wheels carrier. It was not an easy task to finally get our SHERPA-on-wheels carrier. When Abbey came home from the shelter, I decided it was necessary to have it for vacation travel. I purchased a carrier with an over-the-shoulder strap, but it was soon obvious she was getting too heavy to be carried comfortably. I had read about the quality of the SHERPA carriers and set out to find one. None of the pet stores in our area (suburban Chicago) had what I wanted. Therefore, I bought what was available, a Samsonite with wheels. On our first trip with this carrier, the wheel broke off at the ticketing counter, and I was stuck with a broken carrier. My next step was to survey the pet catalogs. I found exactly what I needed and wanted in SHERPA. It has been used on each trip thereafter and is of the quality I expected.

Thank you for persuading the airlines to allow animals to travel.

Lorraine C.

Over the years, I have received thousands of letters like this one accompanied by adorably wonderful photos of pets traveling in their SHERPA Bags. Each letter was unique and always inspired me to do more. The SHERPA photo contest was a huge success and furthered my mission more on educating and familiarizing people on pet travel. I loved the photos, the letters, and the affirmations that what I was doing what I was meant to do. When you read the heartfelt sincerity in these letters, it's impossible not to feel that you have created a wonderful feeling of belonging to a loving community of pet lovers—from a marketing and sales perspective, it deeply escalated our wonderful world by touching people's hearts, and being involved with their beloved four-legged companions.

Everyone believed and gave me such positive aspirations; our loving community kept growing. In today's world of smart phones, Instagram, and digital technology, it is so much easier to get the word and photos shared and downloaded. We have come a long way technologically, as we all know. Nonetheless, the core concept of what I created remains relevant: you must connect to your market in a meaningful, purposeful way. A product is just a product until you make sure it favorably impacts people's lives.

The SHERPA Bag was always more than just a bag. It was a lifestyle and a way to connect with a community of like-minded people and their pets. The product or service you create must be a lifelong endeavor to help the world be a better place. Think of all the things in your life that you feel truly connected to and love to do. My philosophy has always been to do what you love, in the places you love with the people and pets you love. Find a way to make your product and brand connect to people on the deepest level of their lives.

As you will recall from Lorraine's note, she mentioned she had purchased a Samsonite carrier. Well, I certainly have a story about that! As I've told you earlier, I started my company in 1988, and at the time, SHERPA was the first and only soft-sided pet carrier in the world. You cannot imagine how overjoyed I was when the CEO of Petco himself said: "Gayle, you created a category." When you create a category, there will inevitably be copies.

Connie and I were working the largest pet product show in the United States in Orlando, Florida. It was such an important show, and I always made sure I was there very early in the morning, shopping to see what was new and what was "not new."

I always made sure to "shop the show" to see what was happening in the marketplace. Well, this time, I was in for a major shock because what was "not new" was, in fact, copies of the SHERPA Bag. What I saw were exact copies of the SHERPA Bag branded under a well-known luggage brand. When I saw these were exact copies of my bags, I wanted to throw up. Such a blatant downright copy was appalling; I was speechless and emotionally in shock. What I soon discovered was that Gertie and her husband had licensed the luggage brand's name and totally copied my designs. Licensing is a common practice in the business world: you pay to have the name of a large, reputable company attached to your product. In this case, the luggage brand was unknowingly lending its credence to this fraudulent copy-cat.

As I said, I thought I was going to throw up. When something really affects me emotionally, I always get sick to my stomach. But I didn't vomit—I called my attorney. What he told me was to get all the information, and we would send a "Cease and Desist" letter. I was in for a fight with really bad people, and I had to do the best I could do and continue on. That day, I didn't confront them. Everyone was shocked to see someone had completely copied the SHERPA Bags. How could they do that? Everyone wanted to know. Well, a few months later, while I was working the Travel Goods Show, a group of five men came up to me and introduced themselves. They told me that they were with a major luggage company and wanted me to know that licensing their brand to Gertie was not their idea and that I had a great product. I did get some satisfaction from their words. Everyone in the industry knew there was only the SHERPA Bag, and I had worked endlessly to change the policy for pets on every major airline in the world.

The major lesson I want to share is simple: In running a business, you must protect yourself in many different ways.

Copy-cats will jump into the market because that's what a cat does: they just jump right in. You must have a great product registration and copyright your brand name. If you've come up with a great idea, people may try to steal it. When someone does copy you—and believe me, they will if you have a great product—a lawsuit would be the first thing to avoid, as it is a lot of time and money. Remember, an idea is nothing; you must always create a different product and lay a very successful foundation. The reality is you must always be five steps ahead of the competition.

The negative experience I just described having at a trade show, where I encountered a copy-cat, certainly became indicative of all shows in the future. Over the years, I have gone to thousands of gift shows, dog shows, trade shows, and expos to promote my companies worldwide. These shows have many wonderful and not so wonderful people I have met and has been very enlightening and rewarding. It was always a painful experience seeing an over-abundance of fake SHERPA Bags all over the world. Now, there is still a proliferation of soft-sided pet carriers. Still, I am and always will be devoted to the products I have created. The dogs and the cats love them, and SHERPA continues to rank number one in every media list of pet carriers.

The Westminster Dog Show, the most prestigious dog show in the United States, then and now, takes place in February in New York City. This is the time New York City "goes to the dogs." The most beautiful, gorgeous, loving animal beings descend upon NYC, filling every hotel that will take pets.

Over the course of a week, a cornucopia of different dog shows take place, culminating in the Westminster Dog Show. The first show of the week is the Pet Fashion Show. In truth, it's a bit over the top, with dogs in ornate costumes of the Marie Antoinette style-high fashion. Still, it is fun to see all the pets in their elaborate outfits.

A show I also love so much occurs the day before, The Progressive Dog Show. A show where I will always come in contact with my wonderful world of animal lovers, breeders, groomers, handlers, and all the people that love animals. When I see these people, I always feel a warm sense of camaraderie and purpose.

The Westminster Dog Show was so exciting to me the first time I walked in thirty-five years ago. My heart and soul felt right at home. "This is where I was meant to be." I would remain there all day and late into the night, talking with the different breeders, groomers, owners, and handlers. Every single breed of dog is at that show in the beginning. To my great joy, I saw many of the smaller dogs being carried around in SHERPA Bags. I heard from so many breeders that my bags were the bag for them—the one they preferred to use. Talk about being proud! These people were at the very pinnacle of our industry and confirmed their love for my product.

Later in the week, we have the Yorkie Specialty Show, which is always at the New Yorker Hotel. I was and continue to be at all these shows, meeting people, meeting dogs, and connecting with my community. I love talking to the groomers, breeders, handlers. Before the dogs can show, they must be totally groomed to perfection. There's a certain specific look, cut, everything, that each breed must-have. This was all so interesting to me. I have always loved it and those wonderful dogs. In the beginning, going to every show to make people aware of the SHERPA Bag was first and foremost in my mind. I was the alternative to the hard plastic carrier, and I had a major workload in front of me. I think about all the different comments when people felt it was cruel to put your dog inside a SHERPA Bag. They could not understand how the dog or cat could breathe, and they also unknowingly felt it was a punishment. I had to show them how and promoting the SHERPA Bag was why I went to these shows, but more than that, it was the connectivity, the pride. This was my world with the animals, a world in which I felt so at home in. They were the reason I put so much time and effort into designing the perfect soft-sided pet carrier. It is imperative that you have positive affirmations from your market to know and value what you are doing. In my case, the audience was in the field of pet travel. Finding your people in your area and getting positive reactions will inspire you, fuel your creativity, and build your confidence in ways you might never have imagined possible. Staying in shape in your mind, body, spirit is one of the biggest tools to help you achieve your goals in your life. My first job just happened to be working at Jack LaLanne's, the first exercise fitness club.

The last anecdote and related advice I want to share with you in this chapter are about being a woman in business. I've already described how the Women of Enterprise Awards in 1997 were a major accomplishment for me. In 1999 I joined the Women's Presidents Organization. You had to do a minimum of $2 million in business to be accepted. I was doing slightly under that at the time, but thankfully they let me in. This organization was a wonderful learning experience for me. These were successful women in business that I could look up to and learn from. I've always been more creative than business-minded. Connie was the one who kept our financial house in order. Learning from women of this stature was a real gift. It was also inspiring to see that we, as women, could make our own way in what was largely a man's world at the time. In some ways and industries, it is still a man's world. Still, the women I met at the Women's Presidents Organization and at other female-centric organizations I joined didn't see limitations or wouldn't let any we did see stop us. We wanted to stake out our own place in the world, and by helping each other realize our individual dreams, we felt we were helping to make the world a better place.

Being a part of these women's organizations not only connected me to a terrific network of women, but it also instilled in me the importance of paying it forward. Here is how that started: it was the early 2000s, and I was at a pet show when I met a woman whose company was small. I introduced her to different people, and over time helped her grow. Doing things like that became part of my mission in life. I wanted to lift people up. Sharing helpful tools to build a business can help so many. Sharing my mistakes, so others don't make the same ones helps even more. It's easy for me to do while I'm at these shows. When everybody helps each other, we all grow. I love that saying: A rising tide lifts all boats. The rising tide is our deepening bond with our pets and other animals, domestic and wild, who need and deserve our protection. Copy-cats are everywhere. Be prepared for them, protect yourself as much as possible, and continue to innovate beyond their imitations. Coming up with a great idea, and laying a very strong foundation is the key. I hope my examples from those years have been helpful. To sum up, here are the lessons you might want to take away from this chapter.

1. Connect to your market in a meaningful way.
2. Create a community.
3. Professional help is always needed. This will inspire you to be the best version of yourself to build the best version of your business.
4. Join organizations that can help you achieve your goals, but not too many, as time is of the essence. Focus!
5. Help those who need help by sharing life and business lessons that serve you well. In paying it forward, try especially to inspire the next generation.
6. Make sure everything you do is aligned with and in service to your mission.

That last lesson is the most important one to follow. I can say it was never easy for me to do, but I was totally devoted to my mission of helping people go to places they love with the pets they love. It is a mission I continue to fight for to this day. I will be devoted to my goal till my last breath. And that kind of resolve would prove necessary to handle what was about to come next. Not all of my days were joyous, triumphant, and rose-colored. There was a lot of terrible greed, jealousy, and betrayal that threatened the very foundation of SHERPA, testing me in so many ways I could never have imagined, and then it only got worse!

Photo Gallery

From the beginning to now

TWA Hostess Graduation 1971

Greeting Passengers

Checking in at JFK

TWA Flight Attendants Strike

Being With Friends During The Strike

Still On Strike. When Will This End...

Baby SHERPA

SHERPA, The Best Model

Connie, SHERPA, Gayle

The First SHERPA Bag 1988

Another Merry Christmas

Travel TV Segment

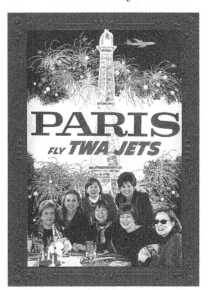

Celebrating With TWA Friends

Flight To The Gulf War - Desert Shield

Boxes In My Bedroom

SuNae & SHERPA Are Happy Travelers

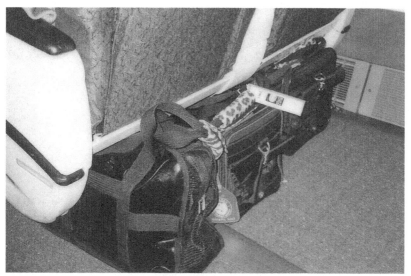

Zipped Up For Travel On Board

*Another
Happy
Traveler*

Winning The Avon & SBA Women Of Enterprise Award

The Great Betty White

Talking About Pet Travel

*Julie & SHERPA Loved
The Travel Collection*

SuNae Was Always True Love

Connie Working in Paris With Me

Bijoux, The Fabulous Birman

SHERPA'S 17th Birthday Extravaganza

Travel First Class With SHERPA

Gare De Lyon, Paris

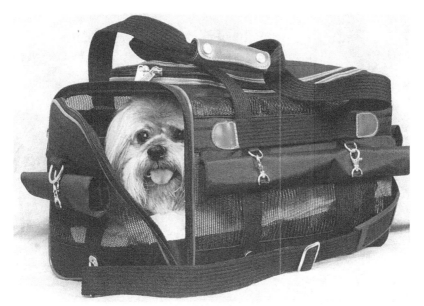

The SHERPA Roll-Up, Traveling Discreetly

SHERPA Pet Trading Company Photo Contest Winners

Photo Shoot with SHERPA

Italian Pet Products Show

Checking-In At CDG, Paris

Almost Ready To Go

SuNae In Her Tote Around Town

SHERPA Was Great At 17

Pet Stop with Brian Voynick, DVM.

Pet Stop Never Stopped

With Wonderful Dr. Brian Voynick

Chicken Or The Egg

Adorable SuNae

Crouch & Fitzgerald With The SHERPA Shop

*The
Wonderful
Crouch &
Fitzgerald
Team*

At The SHERPA Shop in Crouch & Fitzgerald

The Minis At Maxim's

Suze Orman, Connie & Me Keeping Our Financial House In Order

Checking-In At Delta Airlines With "The Girls"

PETCO Meeting At Their Headquarters

SuNae & SHERPA Were Always Elegant Models

Delta Airlines Pet Carrier By SHERPA Was A Winner For Cats & Dogs

Working With Connie On The Champs-Élysées, Paris

SHERPA & SuNae MINIS

The Girls Traveling Around Town In Germany

57th Street In NYC   *Working In Prague, The Czech Republic*

At My Warehouse In Brussels, Belgium

More Boxes And SHERPA Bags In Belgium Warehouse

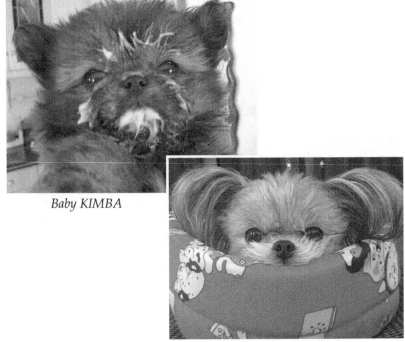

Baby KIMBA

Became The Joy Of My Life

Chris & KIMBA

KIMBA, A True Professional

KIMBA Loved Bernadette Peters

Gayle, KARTU & The Icon, Pearl Nelson

Checking In With Delta Airlines

Happy SHERPA Customers

The Travel Collection With the SHERPA Team

KIMBA Loved her SHERPA Tote

SHERPA Travel Collection Painting

My Best Girls Were The Best Models

105

Enjoying The View In Their SHERPA Tote-Around-Town

KARTU Being Happy

Crouch & Fitzgerald

Best Friends Forever

*Another Check-In
With Overweight
Luggage!*

KIMBA Was A Star In Every Way

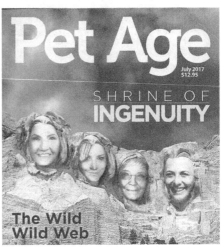

No Pet Left Behind　　*Mount Rushmore Of Award Recipients*

Westminster Dog Show NYC   *Dogs & Cats At Paris Show*

KARTU & KIMBA Always Best Friends

Portrait By David Strano

*KoKo Is
A Star
Already*

*KoKo Loves Being A Pretty Little Girl Next
To A Champion Great Dane*

It's in the Bag

Chapter 6

Shark Attacks:
Jealousy, Greed and Betrayal

2007

Success in business, and the attention that comes along with it, can be a double-edged sword. On the one side, you have all the abundance that success creates: in my case, by 1997 SHERPA Pet Trading Company employed dozens of people and had helped thousands travel safely and comfortably with their pets. This created many positives in my life and the lives of many others. Over the next decade, I continued to appear on television and radio, and be featured in magazines and catalogs. I sold hundreds of thousands of SHERPA Bags, and became a recognized global advocate and spokesperson for improved pet travel. I had found what I was meant to do in the world. My vision for my company's continued growth and development was a continuing process.

However, there was another, more sinister, side: the difficulties caused by the evil, dog-eat-dog aspects of the business world was a sharp sword indeed. Unfortunately, when many eyes are focused on you, not everyone has your best interests in mind. In fact, as I discovered in my naiveté, many of those eyes were green with jealousy. Some people will want what you have; others will actively try to take it away from you. That is exactly what happened to me and the SHERPA business that I had created.

This chapter deals with what happened to me. I believe it is an informative lesson on how greed and jealousy can destroy your business and perhaps even you, since stress kills. People I completely trusted tried to take my business away from me. This is a painful but important subject that will hopefully help you think about how to avoid individuals who hurt more than help. I certainly didn't have the right level of awareness when it happened, and I paid a very big price. Connie and I were overloaded with our day-to-day projects to keep the company going. I was naive toward the evils that existed in the business world, where wolves in sheep's clothing can be not only dangerous to everything you've worked so hard for, but even fatal. If you fail to protect yourself properly, you risk losing everything. You must be totally aware that anything can happen, and cognizant of the earliest signs so that you're not caught by surprise, as I was.

To understand what happened to me and to my business and why I use the metaphor of sharks in the water, you first have to know how a shark hunts. Sharks have highly developed senses that allow them to detect even the most minuscule clues that a prey might be near. Sharks are usually colored to blend in with the ocean floor, making them almost impossible to spot. A shark's sense of smell is so acute that they can detect the presence of a single drop of blood in an area the size of an Olympic swimming pool. Once a shark has tracked down his prey, he stalks it before going in for the kill. Once he's ready, a shark will strike quickly, attempting to debilitate his victim with a single bite. We all remember the movie *Jaws*.

While sharks are normally solitary hunters, they sometimes form groups to hunt, especially when hunting larger fish. The behaviors of these ancient aquatic killers seemed to be mirrored by the men who tried to take my business from me. They fooled me, and Connie as well, completely, and I consider them true con men in every sense of the word. We made the mistake of trusting them. It was a mistake I will never forget, since it has cost me dearly. We all make mistakes—this was my biggest one. I will never forget those sharks and the lessons I learned.

Like the shark activities I just described, these human sharks must have sensed blood in the water when SHERPA reached the top of the pet industry, and they began swimming towards me. I had become a public figure, with SHERPA Bags being sold all over the world, endorsed by celebrities. My concept of safe, comfortable and stylish pet travel was taking off in exciting ways. Busily growing SHERPA, night and day, I was always thinking of new ways the SHERPA brand could expand into an even larger global market.

At that time, my expansion strategy included an exciting new acquisition: the legendary luxury luggage brand Crouch and Fitzgerald. In 2007 an employee at SHERPA named David, who over the years had become my right-hand man, told me that Crouch and Fitzgerald was looking for a buyer. He had worked at that company some years back and was still familiar with its inner workings. I had long admired the brand. The company had an impeccable, storied history stretching back to 1839. In 1890, it had over two hundred workers on Maiden Lane in New York City. Can you imagine two hundred workers in 1890 in New York City? It was known that the Kennedys, the Roosevelts, and even Marilyn Monroe had traveled with the company's trunks and luggage.

Acquiring an ownership interest in Crouch and Fitzgerald was a logical extension of my business, since it had always been a goal of mine to do my own luggage line with SHERPA. I find luggage fascinating, and as a former flight attendant I am a well versed in the luggage category. I wanted the SHERPA brand to be able to provide absolutely everything people would need while traveling, for their pets and for themselves. SHERPA was the brand that finally changed the way that people could travel with their pet. Instead of a logistical hassle, taking your pet along on a trip would be totally natural, something people didn't need to think twice about because now you could travel with your pet safely around town, in a car, on a plane, and for all modes of transportation. I believed that it would make sense for people to buy luggage for themselves and their pets from the same company.

Acquiring an interest in Crouch and Fitzgerald also immediately put me into the high-end luggage marketplace. I also wanted to develop an extensive women's travel collection, including briefcases for women, since they only offered men's briefcases. Back then, being a woman in the business world was totally different. There was nothing like the #MeToo movement, no resources like social media to provide connection, and attitudes toward women in positions of power were largely dismissive. Sadly, respect and professionalism were all too often the exception rather than the norm. While over the years this discrimination has become less overt, we women are still so far behind. It is with greater awareness and work that women are moving to a higher level in the business world.

People took me seriously because I worked hard to inform and teach them how to travel with their pets. That was what I totally believed in. I was a member of the Women's President Organization, the Women's Business Economic National Council, and other women's groups. It was very important for me to be working with women and for all of us to learn how to do better in the business world. I felt that, as a woman, becoming an owner of Crouch and Fitzgerald, and then creating products for women, would be a step forward in the right direction. I needed to design and create great handbags, purses and business bags for women in business, as many women were getting into the business world for the first time, and

Crouch and Fitzgerald had primarily been a brand for men.

A very impressive woman to read about, Mary Kay, was far ahead of her time. She empowered women by putting them in control of their own financial future. There was so much inequality in the workplace that she wanted to help effect change for all women when she launched her business in 1963.

One final element cemented the Crouch & Fitzgerald deal for me: the company's beautiful store on Madison Avenue, which made it perfect. SHERPA pet carriers could finally have a SHERPA shop inside C&F to showcase my existing as well as new bags in that very prestigious location. Once I took over, we had a very successful reopening party at the store. SHERPA the dog was the real spokes-dog in attendance for the new SHERPA section. It was written up in a major gossip column in the New York Post by none other than Cindy Adams.

SHERPA and I had come a long way together. From my tiny studio apartment, to a warehouse in Queens, and now to the gilded streets of Madison Avenue. Becoming an owner of Crouch and Fitzgerald was something I knew I just had to do. I had some of the best professional employees, very talented and wonderful women and men. I kept working to grow the SHERPA brand into new markets, in the United States and Europe. I had opened a small office in Paris, and our product was in many different high-end stores, as I described earlier. Europe was proving to be a very profitable market for SHERPA and was absolutely necessary in building a global brand. Of course, the European market opened up a whole new encyclopedia of rules, regulations and laws. I had many things to learn and made many mistakes along the way but continued to successfully grow the SHERPA brand.

The reason I'm telling you all of this about SHERPA's development and our various ventures during this period is not to pat myself on the back: it's to show you that the things I was doing attracted the attention of the business world. As I reported in the last chapter, I had received an offer to buy my company for four and a half million dollars in 1997 and had turned it down. But then, in 2008, another company in the pet products arena, which I'll refer to as "The Idaho Potato Company," made me another offer. They wanted full acquisition of SHERPA. They were a large company and were offering even more serious money. I considered this offer because they assured me that I could stay on, designing and producing luxury bags and products while they would handle the day-to-day operations of the company. This seemed like a good arrangement, similar to how Vera Wang's company was bought by Target and she was able to design bags and clothing and maintain a high-fashion brand. My thought was that with this arrangement I would have the best of both worlds. SHERPA would continue its growth in the big box super stores and boutique pet stores all over the world, and I would have more time and freedom to design high-end merchandise and continue being an advocate and spokesperson for pet travel and animal welfare.

Before I sold the company I had worked so hard to create, I wanted to work hand in hand with The Idaho Potato Company for a time to "test the waters." That's how I met one of the biggest "potato heads" I had ever encountered, a man I'll refer to as "Bernie Bundt."

Bernie was the head of dog products at The Idaho Potato Company, so he was my point of contact in our day-to-day operations, along with attorneys and other people within the company. When I first met him, he seemed like a good person. He was from Cleveland, Ohio, and was married with children. I thought, okay, he's married, he's from a small town, and he should have had a good upbringing. I trusted him. *Boy did he have me fooled!*

After working together for a while, Bernie told me that he

was leaving The Idaho Potato Company. He advised me to not sell SHERPA and to keep control of the company myself, but to get someone else to run the daily operations. That made sense: with a seasoned executive taking on oversight of day to day business operations, I could keep implementing my singular vision for the brand, with more time to spend in Europe developing SHERPA international and pursuing the other work I did with design and photography.

When Bernie Bundt suggested that he should be the one to run SHERPA's operations, I agreed. It made sense to me and to Connie. I had no indication of the kind of man I later found him to be, or the kind of evil of which I later concluded he was capable of. Since I knew he had passed all the psychological testing they do before hiring anyone at The Idaho Potato Company, I assumed that he had to be perfect. It was decided that Bernie Bundt would be the COO of SHERPA. It was also his suggestion that his business associate, a man I will call "Louie Lutz," would be SHERPA's CFO. I met with Louie and Bernie extensively during this period. Both of them seemed like ethical businessmen. Only later did I come to the conclusion that they were scammers and con men! Unfortunately, Connie and I didn't see that at the time. As I said, the main thing that made me trust Bernie in particular was that he had such a highly-esteemed position at The Idaho Potato Company—a thirty-one million dollar business. Based on his passing their psychological testing and other due diligence, and his apparently being successful while working there, I reasoned that he must be fine. Surely, that company would not have hired him and kept him on if he was not competent and trustworthy.

At first, things seemed fine. Both men were running daily operations while I focused on building SHERPA International, designing women's bags, making contacts at women's organizations, and responding to all of the great publicity, interviews, and TV shows. I had many important accounts in Europe and needed to be there to support them and show them what SHERPA was all about. Harrods of London in particular was so very prestigious, exactly where SHERPA needed to be. I had an experience there I will never forget. I was at the candy section, buying that wonderful English candy, Humbugs that I loved. I had set my beautiful LANVIN purse down next to my feet. Inside was my Cartier wallet, money, my passport and makeup. I looked up at the saleswoman to request my bag of Humbugs. I looked down to pick up my purse to pay and it was no longer there. *No, no, no, this couldn't be happening.* I soon found out that there was a major ring of professional thieves stealing in Harrods. Well, to make a shocking story short, Harrods gave me the money to take a taxi back to my hotel. The next day, when I was flying back to New York City as a TWA Hostess, the airline did everything for me to get a temporary passport so I could leave the country. Life has many facets you must be aware of. One in particular, is to make sure you protect your personal items. In business, stealing is a common practice, and you must make absolutely sure you protect everything. P.S. I still eat Humbugs occasionally, but I now buy them at Marks and Spencer. Oh, I never set my handbag on the floor again.

Back to my business with SHERPA. As I've related, I had been working with different markets. In the beginning, SHERPA, was in Bloomingdales, Macys, Saks Fifth Avenue, Hammacher Schlemmer, and the Ritz Hotel, along with many other prestigious accounts. I was also dealing with the gift market and had gift shows to attend. I was dealing with premium and promotional product expos, so I had those shows and events to plan for in order to exhibit and sell SHERPA Bags. I was working long and hard every day and every night to keep building the SHERPA brand in every market. Groomers and veterinarians were definitely another huge market we were in. In short, I was extremely busy, and I trusted Bernie Bundt and Louie Lutz to do *their* jobs.

One day, a day that I will never forget, Connie and I were together at a domestic pet product show, doing our usual thing. Bernie and Louie flew out to meet us, saying that they wanted to discuss some aspect of the business. This was a bit unusual: Bernie sometimes came to the pet shows, but Louie usually stayed in the office. At the show, they offered to help me further by taking over even more of SHERPA's operations. They said they had many solid business ideas, including how we could move to new warehouse facilities they would manage to get at a lower cost.

Connie and I both thought this would help us in our fabulous continuing growth. We needed help, and this sounded like a good idea. Connie was always for anything that would help me and lighten my overburdened load. She had met both men and seemed to trust them. Connie was very skeptical by nature. She had never been fooled or made mistakes in choosing people to work with. She was an excellent judge of character. After all, she was involved with bookkeeping and financials, and if there were some muddy waters we were getting into, Connie would know about it. When your financial house is not in total order, trouble comes knocking on your door. So far, there had not been any red flags, and she thought this idea would be good for the business.

As I said, Connie and I were exhibiting at a pet product show that day. After Bernie and Louie made their pitch about the company's operations and warehousing needs, they wanted me immediately to sign documents they had already prepared and brought with them. In fact, they had a whole *folder* of documents that they said needed my signature. I initially declined, saying, "I really cannot sign anything without my attorney's approval. He will have to go over these documents and make sure everything was written up exactly the way it should be." They told me the attorney could go over the documents and we could change them, but they needed me to sign that day so they could move forward. They made it seem as if these documents were only necessary for the new operations they would be assuming, such as warehousing, shipping, billing and collecting from the people who didn't pay. They assured me my attorney could go over the documents, and if needed, we could change things later. So I signed! I know, I shouldn't have. It's a cliché, but hindsight *is* 20/20.`

When my attorney read over what I had signed, he was very disturbed. He shook his head and told me that I shouldn't have signed any of the documents. Of course, as you've guessed, I was not able to change anything, as Bernie and Louie had assured me I could. There would be no changing anything at *any* time! I wasn't initially aware that I had made the biggest mistake of my business life, but within six months, I was essentially removed from my own business. The documents I had signed basically gave them complete control of every aspect of operations.

In learning how to deal with business, I always threw myself right into the fire and managed to get out without being burned. This was not one of those times. One of the most important lessons I want to share with you is to never, ever sign anything without an attorney present, or without going over the documents before they are signed. I definitely learned a very painful lesson and will never sign anything without my attorney going over every detail and explaining to me all the legalese and implications.

When my attorney first went over the documents, I told him that Bernie and Louie had said we could change things if we needed to, but it became clear in every cell of my body, and in the pit of my stomach, that what they had done could be the death of me. My vision and mission for SHERPA was going to be greatly compromised. I was devastated. The actions of these two men took a disastrous toll on both my and Connie's life.

To my shock and horror, my attorney told me, as gently as he could, that the contracts I had signed were serious legal documents that could not simply be disregarded. Bernie and Louie didn't waste any time taking total control of every aspect of the SHERPA business. Very quickly, they moved the operations from the Bronx, in New York City, to a large warehouse in Connecticut. I knew something was drastically wrong when I went to the new warehouse and was not allowed in. I was told that I needed signed permission to enter. What the . . . was going on? The nightmare was consuming every part of me. Louie Lutz, as I later concluded, was a rageaholic. Every time I tried to talk to him about the operations and what he was doing, he would yell and scream at me. Bottom line, he had no interest in hearing anything I had to say: he simply wanted to assume control of SHERPA for himself and Bernie Bundt. After a while, Bernie and I couldn't even look at each other. I had to watch hopelessly from the sidelines as everything was moving into directions that were totally out of my control. Soon my fabulous executive offices in New York City were mostly empty. Everything and everyone had been moved to Connecticut. Guess who was left holding the bill for all this expensive office space that was now no longer being used? Me, of course! They didn't help me try to get out of it, they just dumped all of this on me, confidently expecting that the difficulties in all of these situations would make me just go away.

But things didn't work out as they had hoped. Although my initial shock and despair was devastating, I continued to pray with intent on how I could right the wrong that I believed had been done. At one point, I threw myself onto the bed and started to cry but was able to pick myself right back up because

I had absolutely no time to waste. I needed to put a plan in place to continue building SHERPA worldwide.

One day, Connie and I went to their office in Connecticut to speak with them. Louie, sitting behind his desk, began to yell at us in the angry and disrespectful manner that seemed to be his normal way. When I say this man acted like a rageaholic, I am not exaggerating. Later, he had to go for anger management training. But at that meeting, he grew more and more enraged, slammed his hands on the desk and then got up to leave the room. Connie, looking at him dead in the eye, pointed her finger at him, and said: "You sit down." Her tone was commanding. Louie did as he had been told. I'll never forget that: how, in that awful moment, Connie was able to take control of a terrible situation. Nonetheless, we were not able to control these two men when we were not there, which was more and more often, as they continued to shut me out of every facet of SHERPA's operations.

Having no other recourse, we, along with my attorney and accountant, decided to take them to court for legal remedy. I can't say too much about the nitty gritty of the court battle, but it cost me a great deal of the time and money that I should have been using to grow SHERPA. Seeing that SHERPA, which I had poured my entire self, heart and soul into for decades, appeared in danger of being *destroyed* made me feel like I was going to die. It was similar to what I felt when I had found my fiancé dead in bed: a total shock; a bad dream from which I couldn't awaken. My stress levels were through the roof! Without my belief in God and the stress relief I received from yoga, I don't know how I would ever have made it.

The professional team I had with me helped me with everything, but to make matters even more difficult, as the face of SHERPA, I could not allow the public to know anything was wrong in the company. I had to present an outward front that made it appear everything was great. I had to keep showing up to events with the usual happy smile on my face. Here's where my training as a flight attendant helped me immensely. On most flights, you have to fly all night long with no sleep, continue working, doing whatever you had to do, looking great and being calm and confident. So even when I was at my lowest point emotionally and financially, I was always dressed perfectly. My dearest friend, George Simonton, a very talented designer, made sure I was always fashion-forward. I neglected to mention that, at TWA in my early twenties, I had studied at Christine Valmy's International School of Esthetics & Cosmetology to be a grooming consultant. I worked with all the professional makeup artists, so my makeup was always perfect. This is another tool I found useful while living in New York City, where I often had my makeup done by the different cosmetic companies, so I was aware of the new trends and looks. When my clothing ensembles and makeup were perfect, it appeared as if things were under control. It's also a form of coping I've spent years perfecting.

While consciously presenting this outward facade, I needed to take care of the turmoil going on inside of me. Two things helped immensely: prayer and therapy. I think that's important for you to know while reading this book that when life gets in your face like this, and you could use professional help, you need to give yourself permission to reach out in those directions. It is so important to realize that when life becomes so difficult, a true remedy may be, as it has been for me, to see a psychiatrist. I needed professional help to learn to learn how to deal with the difficult situations I was facing with my business. My psychiatrist, Dr. Loizzo, was brilliant and used the 12 Steps, to help me with my difficult business situations. The one step in particular I will never forget was that I admitted I was powerless over being nice, and my business life had become unmanageable.

In fact, you owe it to yourself *and* your business to implement whatever tools are needed to move forward in a healthy way. Therapy, meditation and yoga helped me greatly to take care of the hurt and frustration in my mind, body, and spirit.

One thing I thought a lot about during this time was how in the world was I going to get my company out of this mess? How could I stop blaming myself for being so foolish and trusting? These questions may be more easily asked than answered, but it's not wise to waste time on sick, negative energy. One must take positive action.

These deplorable men saw the success I was having and wanted it for themselves without having to do the kind of work I had done. Jealousy and greed are a sickness. When someone lacks talent, drive, and creativity, he may consider it easier to steal someone else's dream rather than try to make his own way in the world. Perhaps Bernie Bundt and Louie Lutz thought that, as a woman, I wouldn't stand up for myself and would not fight for what was mine. Well, they couldn't have been more wrong about that.

Connie knew and saw the major stress I was under. This had a tremendously negative effect on her, which ultimately led to her having a major stroke. She was at home in California, and I was back in New York City when it happened. Of course, I got on the first plane and flew to her. What I found was horrific: she was totally paralyzed, couldn't get out of bed, and obviously could not walk or talk. This was beyond imagining. She was everything to me. Not only my mother but also my best friend, business partner, financial guru, and everything. The financial house of SHERPA had always been totally in order, and this was due to Connie. Seeing her like this layered clouds of depression and sadness over me. When you love and believe in someone so much, it's one of the most painful and helpless feelings in the world to see them so incapacitated.

Now on top of the ongoing legal battles, and my still being the public face of SHERPA, I became Connie's "Director of Nursing and Healthcare." My goal was to bring her totally back to the fabulous condition she had been in, and this took years. Connie was deeply committed to getting herself back in shape, both mentally and physically. She was always sporty and worked so hard to overcome the debilitation the stroke had caused.

This was one of those time periods we had sometimes been forced to power through, when everything that could go wrong did go wrong. But we managed to get through it together. Connie was an incredibly strong, resilient person. She worked at it every single night and day, and little by little she made unbelievable progress, as only she could. I still remember her going to the courthouse with me, for depositions, in her wheelchair. She was a fighter through and through.

Connie having had a stroke put things in a new dimension. These two men had already achieved part of their diabolical plan. I now had a choice. I could go on endlessly trying to fight them in court, spending a fortune of money, or I could look at the problem in a different light. Yes, the day-to-day operations of SHERPA now appeared greatly compromised, and my vision for SHERPA as a very successful global brand was totally interrupted. Still, that didn't mean I could not or should not continue the important work I was doing as the ambassador for pet travel and SHERPA. For me, education and awareness were always my main objectives. So, with the help of my attorney, I settled the lawsuit on new business terms that I considered more appropriate financially, in exchange for which I agreed to step away from the operations but for a period of time that was far shorter than in the original contracts that I had foolishly signed. I focused on what I had always done best: public relations, outreach, advocacy, and media. SHERPA, the dog was the very best model in photography and the greatest star of all. With my direction, she just knew how to pose perfectly. Bernie Bundt and Louie Lutz had no sovereignty over me in those areas, so I could be exactly who I was meant to be and do what I was meant to do in the public relations arena.

I had a full agenda and was totally committed. I was not going to allow two men whom I found to be mere con artists, or anyone like them, to come into the marketplace to destroy my spirit. It was important to me during this trying time to keep my mind, body, spirit, and sense of self intact. I was able to do that because of a dog named SHERPA. From our earliest days together, SHERPA had always helped me with everything I was doing. When I temporarily lost confidence in myself, SHERPA helped me get my confidence back by giving me the unconditional love that only a dog can give. I would never be where I am today without my precious SHERPA.

Thankfully, this turbulent time in my life did not last forever, but it clearly took a major toll on both Connie and me. Being prepared is paramount with everything you do in life. The love I had received from Connie and SHERPA, along with all of my wonderfully supportive friends, customers, and others who believed in what I was doing, helped me emerge from this torrential storm. I worked so hard to learn how to build a business into a number one global brand. The purpose that drove me was so powerful and uncompromising that it gave me the courage to keep going and continue building the SHERPA brand worldwide. I was determined to swim to shore, out of the reach of sharks and the potato heads.

You won't believe what happened next. Tom Terrific, the white knight, came galloping in with his worldly and wise team to save me, and to rid me of Bernie Bundt and Louie Lutz forever. But that is another story to tell.

Chapter 7

Paris, My European Home

I have loved Paris, "The City of Light," since my very first trip as a young woman more than fifty years ago and will continue to love it until my last day on Earth. It is a city that fills my heart and soul in every way and ignites a burning energy in me to be alive in the truest sense of the word.

Among the lyrics in Cole Porter's classic song, *I Love Paris*, he writes: *I love Paris in the springtime. I love Paris in the fall. I love Paris in the winter when it drizzles, I love Paris in the summer when it sizzles.* Whenever I hear this song, most notably sung over the decades by Ella Fitzgerald and Doris Day, I have to smile, but I must confess, I do not share Cole Porter's loyalty to the city during the blistering hot summers and the freezing winters. I spend those months working at my home in San Clemente, California, in New York, or travelling to different shows I must attend. My dogs KARTU and KoKo are always with me.

My apartment in Paris overlooks the Seine River and has a stunning view of the city's 4th arrondissement. Just before sunset, the light over the river dims to a honey-colored hue, turning to a vibrant red, imbuing the scene with a shimmering atmosphere that stops just short of magic. Through my three large windows, I can gaze out in awe at the beauty and history of my favorite place to be in the world.

Looking out the windows, I would see the beauty of the boats passing by during the day, and lighting up the sky during the night. This is an absolutely exquisite view filled with activity

129

and people passing by when, walking along the Seine, I would see the *bouquinistes*, the local name for sellers of used books, plying their wares from green kiosks that line the banks all the way to the entrance of the Louvre. I once heard a BBC radio program describe the Seine as "the only river in the world that runs between two bookshelves."

Until recently, I was always working in Paris, March through June, enjoying the magnificence of what my favorite city has to offer: the incredible history, the fashion, jewelry, fabric, photo and art shows. Because of the nine-hour time difference with California, I am able to do all the shows during the day and in the late afternoon and evening, I begin working with the United States. When I'm over there, I spend the majority of my time working from my worktable filled with computers, papers and projects while my beloved Shih Tzu, KARTU is usually wandering around or playing with her many toys.

In the spring, I would venture into the city in the late morning, shopping every market in every arrondissement that pertained to what I was working on. I was always shopping to discover new trends, new ideas, and new ways to create. I worked tirelessly in Paris. The nine-hour time difference between Paris and California gave me the feeling that I had an extra nine hours in every day.

My absolute favorite time to be in Paris is in the fall, when all of the fashion world is in full swing. In that season, I feel as though I am completely and totally surrounded by the beauty of the city, with the leaves changing colors and the many fashion shows with gorgeous models walking the runways. How fortunate I was to know where every single market and every show was for fabric, zippers, buttons, trims, appliqué. The name of the game was fashion.

Most of all, I have the feeling of just "being there," a term of my own invention which to me perfectly describes a state of being truly present in your life. It is that moment or time when the place where you are, the physical surroundings, exactly match how you feel inside. That feeling of being there doesn't *only* happen to me in Paris, but it happens to me most often in Paris. I could be doing something as simple as watching people buy an ice cream at the esteemed *glacier* Berthillon and slowly enjoy their unbelievable ice cream. I feel as though I am experiencing the city, and myself, totally, feeling at home.

With this concept of "being there" foremost in my mind, I want to share with you some of the useful lessons this city has taught me over the fifty years I have called it my second home. Whether you are interested in expanding your personal horizons through travel, thinking about embarking on a creative endeavor, looking to deepen your spirituality, or simply feel you need to shake things up and head in a new direction, Paris and Europe really have something to teach you. Beauty and wisdom are a potent combination for growth, and beautiful Paris, a city that has taught me so much, is also one of the most profound, educational, magnificent, historical and inspirational cities on earth.

***

Diving Right Into What's Right For You

I first arrived in Paris in 1971. At the time, I was working as a hostess for TWA. I was scheduled to work a flight that was departing from John F. Kennedy Airport in New York and arriving at *Charles De Gaulle Airport* in Paris. From the moment I stepped off the plane, the city filled me with a sense of belonging. The immediate connection awakened a need to discover all of the bountiful beauty Paris had to offer. I wanted to see and do everything, view every piece of art, shop every store, walk down every avenue, take in every fashion show, and note every trend.

Unfortunately, though, that layover was a short one. I rarely had forty-eight hours in Paris before I had to turn around and fly home to New York City. How could I "do it all" in such a short amount of time? Anyone who knows me knows that not "doing it all" was never an option. That first trip I was so excited I could not sleep and ventured off to learn as much as I could. I needed to discover Paris and absolutely loved it.

This was the era of Julia Child, when French cooking and interest in French food was at an all-time high. Who cared what butter and cream did to our bodies? I cared far more about learning all of the aspects of preparing and knowing about French cuisine. Every ingredient can be found in the marketplaces of Paris. Interestingly, French people, as a rule, are slender, even though they love their French baguettes and other food that is so rich, succulent and so exquisitely prepared, that one doesn't have to eat large portions. My infatuation with French cuisine turned out to be a long affair. Years later I studied culinary arts at the famous Parisian cooking school La Varenne as well as with the famous chef and cookbook author, Janeen Sarlin, at her school in New York City, called Cooking With Class.

The 24-hour layover began a now more than fifty-year love affair with Paris. I had found something special and never looked back. Embarking with great delight into this new experience was one of the best decisions I ever made. I can't possibly *imagine* my life without Paris.

As you navigate the waters of your own life, don't be afraid to dive into something new—with a big splash! If something feels Right with a capital R, you will know it in that moment. It could be a new job, moving to a new city, a fledgling relationship, or wanting to simply experience something new. Be decisive. Trust your heart. Trepidation and doubt are your enemies, while an open mind and open arms are your allies. Approach new experiences fearlessly, and the universe will generously reward you.

***

Finding a Spiritual Soulmate

Some of my favorite memories of Paris are the times I spent with my best friend and spiritual soulmate **Leslie,** I met Leslie in the 1990s at a dinner thrown by the Delta Society, the first and premier nonprofit registry for therapy dogs and other therapy animals, including, cats, horses, and other species. The Delta Society incidentally is now called Pet Partners and still does marvelous work. We became extremely close. She was from a well-to-do family and could afford to spend lots of time with me overseas as I worked to build the SHERPA brand in Europe. She was totally emotionally supportive of me during all those turbulent times with the sharks in the water and the snakes in the grass.

The time I spent in Paris with Leslie was always priceless to me. Sometimes we would stay in boutique hotels with adjoining doors to our rooms. Over late lunches in small cafes, we talked about everything in our lives. Sometimes, we would take a little trip down to the southern coast and explore towns like Sainte Maxime. We were both Catholics and often discussed our faith together, which only deepened our bond. Leslie knew all the words to the prayers and masses by heart, which always impressed me. She was well-traveled, had interesting friends, could speak French, and was a real woman of the world. She also liked to sleep late, so our first meal of the day was usually a late lunch at three-thirty in the afternoon. How European of us! We had a great life together, we really did.

Sadly, Leslie passed away in 2019, but she is not gone from my heart, my soul or my thoughts as she is always with me. Leslie was the truest, most loving friend, and our time together was priceless and filled with joy. She just accepted me unconditionally. That is such a powerful emotion to feel from a friend, especially if you are both in the prime of your lives in the city of your dreams.

My advice to you would be to make sure you have at least one person in your life whom you consider a spiritual soulmate and who accepts you exactly for who you are. That person can of course be a romantic partner, or the platonic friendship I had with Leslie. This relationship will allow you to blossom. Support is such an essential part of any endeavor you undertake—especially emotional support.

One thing to remember: intense friendships like this are a two-way street. If you are lucky enough to find someone special, make sure you let them know, emphatically, that you are their biggest fan, just as they are for you. Pay attention to their feelings, and make sure they feel seen and heard. With Leslie, it was always easy, she was such a beacon of light in my life.

***

Deepen Your Faith

Never do I feel more connected to God than I do in Paris. For one thing the cathedrals are among the most beautiful in the world. *Notre Dame, Sainte-Clotilde, Chartes,* all these icons of religious architecture filled me with awe. I also love the smaller though no less holy cathedrals near my apartment. I usually walk through their doors in the late afternoon and a feeling of peace and calm comes over me. Often, they are nearly empty. Their magnificent sculptures and towering organ pipes sit in silence, or a lone priest intones softly behind the pulpit. I will light a candle, or simply pray quietly. It gives me peace in my heart and soul. For me, prayer all comes down the concept of intent. When you pray, you must pray with intent. You must know what you are doing and why you are doing it. When you want to do great things, you will be able to do great things.

My faith has always been an important part of my life, especially my journey with SHERPA. Although, being baptized as a Catholic and I follow under that set of doctrines, I think the role that spirituality plays in my life can be applied universally to anyone who believes in a power greater than themselves. Yours may be entirely different, but the central point remains the same. Find *your* own version of the cathedrals of Paris. It might be a local church, it might be a park, and it might be the beach--any place that feels "holy" to you. When you are there, try to connect to your spiritual side in a meaningful way. Pray with intent. I promise that you will grow as a person as a result.

***

When Life Changes, You Must Change

In March of 2020, something happened that would change my relationship with the city of Paris. More accurately, something happened that would change the reality globally. I am of course speaking of the Coronavirus outbreak that spiraled out of control over the early months of 2020, when the world quite literally shut down for a protracted period of time, causing multi-millions of illnesses globally and over a million deaths of men, women, and even young children as scientists worldwide desperately worked on trying to develop a vaccine.

When the news first hit, I was at my home in San Clemente, California. Like most Americans, I monitored the reports closely, increasingly aghast as the situation rapidly worsened. I had already booked tickets and was set to return to Paris in a few days. As usual, I planned to spend the spring months working in Paris and spending quality time with KARTU, and my adorable, joy of my life, KoKo, the newest addition to my pet family. She is a Mi-Ki, the same breed as KIMBA, who was KoKo's renowned predecessor. The Mi-Ki is a new breed combining the best traits of a Japanese Chin, a Maltese, and a Papillon. I also planned to attend a number of pet product shows throughout the season, including the largest one, held each year in Nuremberg, Germany.

As I watched the number of Coronavirus infections, and deaths, tick steadily upwards worldwide, I knew that my travel plans were dead in the water. This was confirmed with absolute certainty on March 15th, when France's Prime Minister Édouard Philippe announced a lockdown of his entire nation. My flight was canceled, and a few days later, Californians were ordered to "shelter in place" by our governor.

From a distance I watched in horror as France began to report hundreds of fatalities. Each day, the death toll mounted. My heart broke for my Paris. I couldn't believe that this place of light, love, music, fashion, history and culture was so horribly struck by an invisible enemy, one that threatened to destroy the Parisian way of life. I imagined Parisians stuck inside, where people, at least for the foreseeable future, could no longer meet up in cafes, listen to music in concert halls, or even gather along the banks of the Seine. Unthinkable! The worst part of this for me, and for all of us, was the uncertainty. You never knew when the news was going to inform you of some new catastrophe, another major alternation of the world as we knew it.

During these trying times, which, let's be frank, felt apocalyptic, I was so glad to be home near the ocean, in my case the Pacific Ocean. Looking out at the waves has always been a source of comfort, but it gained special significance for me during this difficult period. I took many solitary walks on the pier, making sure to "social distance" from anyone I encountered. The ocean looked bluer and more beautiful than usual, contrasting starkly against the dark and dreary social backdrop.

Gazing at the water, something stirred in my mind. I began to think about the future, specifically *my* future, in a new way.

I had to face the realization that the world might not go back to the way it was for a very long time, and perhaps not ever. What kind of Paris would I be returning to? The world had tilted on its axis. I had no choice but to tilt with it, and try to adjust to this new reality. Changez la vie… Change the life!

The lease on my Paris apartment – I had sold my first apartment and had been renting the one next door—was up on May 1, 2020. On one of my walks on the San Clemente pier, I made the decision that I would keep my apartment. I've always been a decisive person, trusting my instincts, and knew that I had made the right decision. Paris would always be there for me, but for now my home and business would have to be centered out of California, the risk of a premature return to France was too great. My health and safety were not negotiable.

While the COVID-19 outbreak was uncharted territory, being in a difficult and ever-changing situation was nothing new for me. As I reminded myself more than once, I had changed with the times before, adapting to difficult circumstances. I found my fiancé dead in bed. I lost my livelihood. I dealt with the fallout when two scoundrels tried to take my business away from me. Trusted employees had stolen from me—a heartbreak to anyone. There was no way I was going to let this virus be the end of me! The priority is to be safe and healthy as we deal with these perilous times.

As with almost everything else, the entire pet travel industry had ground to a halt. Everyone was going to lose a significant amount of business that would have been generated from that spring's trade shows, events, and promotions. Everything I had worked for over the last three decades was changing, due to the drastic slowdown in travel overall.

Right now, the entire world is at a critical juncture. My mind works well in a crisis. I'm able to adapt, improvise, and overcome. I thought about what I could do to help make a difference in the current situation. Everyone was so disturbed, so far from peace, I knew I needed to make some sort of public statement that spoke to this particular time and offered comfort and assistance.

Under my Gayle Martz, Inc., I had warehoused a large amount of fashionable bags. These included such great items as the *Tote on Wheels* and *The Sling Bag*. Since I now wouldn't have an opportunity to market these items at trade shows, I needed to "go digital" to boost my online sales. My thought was to move a significant amount of bags through online sales in order to generate income for my business during this difficult time, using that to raise money to donate to worthy pet-related causes. Perhaps I would also be able to help people and pets in Paris in this great time of need.

Over the next several weeks, I thought to build out my online portal, up my online marketing presence, and sell my inventory. Because of the circumstances, that never happened, as this terrible health and economic crisis steamrolled through our lives and, I was grateful to donate all of my inventory to The Greater Good Charities, that protects people, pets and the planet. Through The Greater Good Charities many of my bags were also donated to The Sato Project charity.

For now, my decision to stop living in Paris for half of each year has reinforced a recurring theme of my career, that when life changes you have to be open and willing to change, or at least willing to live with your fears and not let them stop you. Every entrepreneur needs to be aware that he or she will always have to adjust to new circumstances. The only thing you can rely on is that the world *will* change. At times such as this, it may be especially difficult when your business and life change in ways that catch you off guard. That's the time you need to stay focused, be able to change, and calculate your next move. If you can do that, you'll survive even the most severe storms.

I don't know when I'll see Paris again, but I know one day

I will. After paying over 50 thousand dollars in rent and not being able to go to Paris, I was advised and knew it was time for me to move out of my rental apartment. Americans are not allowed to enter France, and many countries and the global pandemic continued to spread and strengthen. My most wonderful, talented European god daughter came from Belgrade to stay with me in Paris even though I wasn't there. She had purchased her ticket before and how grateful I was that she could be in my apartment and told me I really must move out. She arranged for a moving company, we went over everything that was mine in the apartment and during a very sleepless night for me, everything was packed up and put into storage. Thanks to the wonders of technology, FaceTime, WhatsApp and other virtual communication--they all allow us to work night and day all over the world. The time difference between California and Paris is nine hours, and I accomplished so much during the middle of the night and was all moved out by the morning. Paris will always continue to be there for all of us. This pandemic may have dimmed her incandescence, but nothing can ever fully extinguish the City of Light's beauty, grace and appeal. It has changed, but in the process of dealing with this threat to our very existence we have also changed. In some ways this trial by fire has made us more precious to each other. This in turn, will, I am hopeful, ultimately allow us to build a better world, and not only for us, but also for the wonderful animal companions that grace our lives.

It's in the Bag

Chapter 8

Pets Are Family: The Dogs in My Life

I am writing the last few chapters of this book in the spring of 2020, when the world is locked away under the Coronavirus quarantine. Eventually in our new world, this horrific virus will pass. I am an optimist, and feel sure there are better days to come. The travel bans and stay-at-home orders will lift. The country will begin, albeit perhaps slowly, to move back into motion. As we continue to help each other remotely as much as we can, people will gradually adjust to the "New Normal." Most of us, at least, have acquired a greater caring emotion for each other and the world due to the loss of freedom and the loss of so many lives.

Traveling has been totally out of the question. We have all been and continue to be, locked down, to help slow the spread of this horrific virus. To keep everyone healthy and safe, we need to adhere to all of the protective protocols. For now, the thought of taking planes and trains, and driving in cars, to visit places far from home with our pets, is out of the question for most of us. I look forward to the time, with all my heart, when this critical nightmare will pass. Since travel for people and their pets has been my life's work, I along with everyone else have been forced to change. We have a lot more work to do to heal and stabilize the world.

With a career that has had me traveling all over the world for the past four decades, I have not been able to spend extended periods of time at my home, in San Clemente, California. I cannot recall the last time I spent months here without getting on a plane. Since the early days of my wanderlust, I have always been on the move. For now, I, like everyone else, am "sheltered in place."

Here in San Clemente, the streets are almost empty and very silent. From my windows I can see the freeway, with very little traffic, which is certainly a rarity. If we go out, a face mask must be worn at all times. In Japan, masks were always worn because the pollution has always been dangerous. Interestingly, pollution levels have gone way down worldwide because people can't go out and there are fewer cars on the road, diminishing pollution causing factors. This has been a dramatic change of life for everyone.

With everything that's going on, I have made a conscious decision to make the best use of my time working inside watching the news twice a day to stay up to date and hear warnings and alerts. I have chosen to stay positive and actively work on staying healthy to build up my immune system. One of the best things for me was having my extremely knowledgeable and talented spine doctor begin a treatment of STIM technology on my aching, badly damaged back. I can highly recommend this treatment as my pain level went from 9 (barely tolerable) to 4 once the procedure took effect. Wonders never cease when we have knowledgeable doctors and nurses who know what they are doing. All of the frontline healthcare professionals and other workers have been a godsend during this global pandemic, and have worked above and beyond their call of duty. Everyone is extremely thankful and grateful for their professionalism and endless comfort and attentive care.

I do get pulled into the ever-churning cable news, but I prefer to use this period of enforced quiet time to write this book, by looking back and then looking forward on my life. Writing this book has always required quiet and solo contemplation, but this extreme quarantine has made me ask myself some big questions. I am actively trying to figure out new ways to donate some of my travel collection and other pet products to those who need them. What else can I really do now to help improve the human-animal bond?

The other day, while working, I was suddenly interrupted by barking from another room. Even without looking, I knew that my adorable three pound puppy, KoKo, had begun playfully torturing KARTU by jumping all over her. KoKo just wants to play and have fun and is still being trained. She can be quite the naughty girl at times. I walked over to distract her with her toys. Positive association always works when training a pet. Scolding and screaming never does. I put KoKo against my heart—where I have always held all my dogs. Weighing only three pounds, she more than makes up for her small size with her loving adoration, her wonderful personality, and is an enormous source of joy for me.

My dogs have always been the most important in my life and brought me the great gift of unconditional love. I could not have gotten through the toughest times in my life the way I did, without them. We have shared many truly important moments together. Creating the first soft-sided pet carrier that was officially approved by major airlines was SHERPA's and my legacy. SHERPA and I worked together to change the pets on board policy with all the major airlines to allow pets in cabins. As part of that initiative, policies had to be changed at each airline since they each had their own rules and regulations.

Holding my little bundle of energy close, I said, "KoKo you are my best little girl. I have a lot of great things in store for you for your future." Putting her down, she immediately scampered off towards her next adventure, and I sat down to go through all the many files pertinent to my business life. I have kept the files and records of my professional life for over thirty years. While

I've been working on this book, I have been searching, finding valuable information, for important files and folders and photos from all the many years of my career and spreading them out everywhere. I am making sure though that an interested dog can't chew and destroy any of it as an eight month old puppy loves to do. I always caution anyone coming into my house to remember one thing: For dogs, anything on the floor belongs to them. There have been so many glasses, headsets, pencils, pens and papers that were bitten up or shredded because I neglected to pick up what was on the floor. In truth, I do my best work on the floor, where I can get into a relaxed and focused state of mind, similar to what I feel when I'm practicing yoga.

Over the last four months I have been discovering and finding so much of my life that is documented in magazine and newspaper articles. Reading over the testimonials and photos of all the beloved four legged and two legged SHERPA community is heart-warming. On my darkest days reading what they have written to me has always picked me up and helped me want to do more. To be willing to work night and day, every day of my life, you must be doing what you love and believe it will make a difference in the world.

All of my beloved companions, SHERPA, SuNae, KARTU, KIMBA and now KoKo have changed my life for the better. I am totally blessed that I found what I was meant to do. Now, reminiscing about my beloved dogs, I'll take you through the most special and profound moments I've shared with each of these five beautiful beings and show you the lessons they have each taught me. As I am sure you'll agree, we can learn as much from our pets as we can from each other, and perhaps even more. These loving beings are angels in disguise. They ask nothing from us but our love, caring, tenderness, and companionship. In return, they give us unconditional love, which is the most valuable gift in the world. Understanding my pets, canine companions, and the role they have had in my life, can give me a better understanding of myself.

SHERPA: The Queen of the Empire and The Star of the Show

From everything you have read so far, you know SHERPA became the defining life-changing factor in my life. I've also already devoted a chapter to how SHERPA came into my life, so I won't repeat myself. Instead, I want to help you get to know her the way I knew her.

If you want to understand what kind of relationship you can expect to have with a particular dog, it's best to start by familiarizing yourself with the characteristics of their breed. SHERPA was a Lhasa Apso. The Lhasa Apso is a non-sporting dog breed, used as an interior sentinel in Buddhist monasteries to alert the monks to any intruders. The ideal Lhasa Apso temperament is being loyal to those closest to them and wary of strangers. Left untrained they can be very aggressive to people they don't know. Lhasa Apsos will let their owners know when they don't want to do something. These dogs require socialization with other dogs and people, as puppies and throughout their lives, because they are an independent and intelligent breed. Standing less than a foot high at the shoulder, they are small, hardy dogs and aristocratic. They're famous for their floor-length flat-hanging coat, parted in the middle and draping all the way down over each side of the body. I kept SHERPA's hair much shorter than this, but she still had a very regal look to her. The windows of a Lhasa's soul are in their deep, oval-shaped eyes. In Tibetan folklore the country's protector is the mythical Snow Lion, and, according to the American Kennel Club, Lhasas, the "bearded lion dogs," are the Snow Lion's earthly representatives.

SHERPA was fiercely loyal, and acted as my protector. Over the seventeen years we spent together she taught me what it was like to be so unconditionally loved. She was always with me and we worked so very hard together. She was by my side for almost two decades as we built our business together.

The hardest lesson SHERPA taught me was how to let go. In 2004, after building SHERPA Pet Trading Company, traveling around the world together, and having countless adventures, SHERPA, at age seventeen couldn't see, couldn't hear and was having trouble walking. She had suffered an injury in an accidental fall some time before and was now in constant pain.

It was extremely difficult for me to accept, but it was time for her to go, and not let her suffer. I knew SHERPA would be waiting for me on Rainbow Bridge. In case you aren't familiar with the concept, it is a heaven for pets that comes from this poem, written anonymously:

Just This Side of Heaven is a Place Called Rainbow Bridge.

When an animal dies that has been especially close to someone here, that pet goes to Rainbow Bridge. There are meadows and hills for all of our special friends so they can run and play together. There is plenty of food, water, and sunshine, and our friends are warm and comfortable.

All the animals who had been ill and old are restored to health and vigor. Those who were hurt or maimed are made whole and strong again, just as we remember them in our dreams of days and times gone by. The animals are happy and content, except for one small thing; they each miss someone very special to them, who had to be left behind.

They all run and play together, but the day comes when one suddenly stops and looks into the distance. His bright eyes are intent. His eager body quivers. Suddenly he begins to

run from the group, flying over the green grass,
his legs carrying him faster and faster.

You have been spotted, and when you and your special friend
finally meet, you cling together in joyous reunion, never
to be parted again. The happy kisses rain upon your
face; your hands again caress the beloved head, and you look
once more into the trusting eyes of your pet, so long gone
from your life but never absent from your heart.

Then you cross Rainbow Bridge together.

Knowing that SHERPA was headed to the Rainbow Bridge was a source of great comfort to me. I couldn't bear her being in pain any longer. I also wanted her to pass with dignity. I've always believed that the ceremonies surrounding our passing to the next world provide gravity and poignancy to the experience, so I had to do the very best I could at this difficult time.

I began by putting music on and lighting candles everywhere, in my home and on the terrace. The veterinarian had already arrived and given SHERPA a tranquilizing treat. She assured me that there would be no discomfort. I wanted an atmosphere of peacefulness to surround us with that calming music and the glow of candle light.

With my other sweet dog, SuNae on my lap, I let both my hands rest on SHERPA as the veterinarian administered the shot that would send her to heaven. Right at that moment, SuNae jumped out of my lap. She knew that SHERPA was already on her way to Rainbow Bridge. These were my last moments with the beloved dog that had started it all.

The vet looked at me, and said, "She's gone." After a moment of reflection and prayer I looked at her, "Now you take her," I said as I put her gently into her favorite SHERPA Bag.

"How will I get this bag back to you?" she asked.

"Please just donate the bag," I said.

Thus began a tradition of my own invention. When the time comes that I have to help send my pet to Rainbow Bridge I always make sure they pass on with total dignity, surrounded by the ones they love. I make sure they have one final trip in their SHERPA Bag, and always donate the bag. Sometimes I wonder if the pet owner who received that first SHERPA Bag knew just how special it was and whether they knew that the queen of the SHERPA empire had once called it home.

I miss SHERPA's love, her personality, and her strength. Dogs that were once guards for Dalai Lamas and monks have to be very special. With SHERPA's strength came a kind of tenderness. I would feel it in the warmth I got from her body as I held her in my arms, against my chest, close to my heart. She is still with me every single day.

SuNae: True Love

SuNae was born in Belgium on September 26, 1996, and I got her from a well known breeder. She was a Coton de Tulear. The Coton de Tulear is the "Royal Dog of Madagascar." The breed is known as bright, happy-go-lucky companion dogs. Their favorite activity is being with the one they love. The Coton is small but robust and sturdy. I thought SuNae would be a perfect companion for SHERPA.

I flew to Brussels on September 13, 1997 to get my new dog. Interestingly, that evening I almost missed my flight, which is something I had never done before. I have always been diligent about getting to the airport early. You must always be when you travel with pets, and especially if you are known as a worldwide ambassador for pet travel, as I can never risk giving pet travel a bad name. What happened that evening is that, sitting in the airline lounge, I checked my watch, and saw that I still had an hour before boarding. I had no idea that my watch had stopped. Suddenly, an airport attendant came running to find me, all out of breath. "Everyone is waiting for you!" he shouted. I looked at my watch and realized the time was the same as the last time I checked. My flight was about to leave. I barely made it on board. Can you imagine if I, whose job it is to teach people how to travel with pets, had missed my flight to get my new pet?

I arrived in Belgium without further incident and met with the breeder, who had originally named SuNae "Sweetie Pie." Of course she had an immediate name change. SuNae means "true love" in Korean. She kissed me the moment she saw me. From that point we were completely bonded. She stayed underneath the seat in front of me in her red SHERPA Bag and kept peering up at me.

When I got back to the states, the first thing I did was introduce SHERPA to her new best friend. SHERPA was ten at the time, and SuNae was just what she needed. I've followed that pattern with all my dogs since. When they turn ten, I introduce a new dog into the family. That way I will always have a dog in my life and my dogs will always have a companion.

If you ever plan to add a second dog to your family, do not bring a new dog into another dog's territory without the proper introduction. On the day I returned from Belgium with SuNae, I had a professional trainer, Bash Dibra, waiting at a local dog park in NYC where I lived at the time with SHERPA. SuNae and I arrived at the park and I introduced them. I was so thrilled to see that they became best friends right away, and we all walked home together.

As a new SHERPA mascot, SuNae had a huge job ahead of her. By that time my company had really taken off, with orders coming in from all over the world. My team and I worked around the clock to make sure the new marketing materials reflected our new brand, which now included SuNae. I spent much of my time writing new copy, and also updating "Travel Tips and Tales" to bring everyone up to date.

Happily, my customers really loved SuNae and could not believe how tiny and wonderful she was. They constantly wrote letters to me about how much they loved her. Pets were finally getting a small amount of recognition for how important they are to us in our lives. SuNae and all the animals inspired me to work extremely hard and be the best at everything I did. It's impossible to overstate the impact she had on my life in my continuing to build the SHERPA brand worldwide.

KARTU: The Jet-Setting Shih Tzu, aka "Miss Attitude"

KARTU was born in Arkansas on September 3, 2006. When you own a Shih Tzu, you own a little bit of Chinese history. Centuries ago, imperial breeders in the palace of the Chinese emperor developed the Shih Tzu from Tibetan breeding stock. The name means "lion dog," as distinct from the Lhasa Apso which translates as a "bearded lion dog." Until the 1930s, the breed remained hidden behind palace walls, virtually unknown to the outside world. Since then, the Shih Tzu has been one of the most popular toy dogs. They also treat their owners like royalty. KARTU certainly thought of herself as royalty.

I think the story of how KARTU came into my life is remarkable, because it shows just how much of an impact I had on changing all the airlines' policies. The breeder was originally supposed to send KARTU from Arkansas to California, in the cargo hold. I really needed help with pets traveling in cargo so people would be more aware of how safe it is for their pet. So many animals must travel in cargo and I wanted to make sure everything was taken care of perfectly, God forbid anything would happen to KARTU on her flight. However, that year the weather was especially cold, and on the day of her plane trip the temperature was too low to safely transport her in cargo. The breeder actually drove out to the airport three different times, and each time KARTU was not permitted in cargo because it was too cold. Pets cannot be accepted in cargo when the ground temperature is below 45 degrees. Of course, when it came to my pet's travel, safety was always paramount. I wanted KARTU with me but resigned myself to the fact that everything had to be perfect in order for her to travel, so I would just have to wait until everything was perfect for her to come to me.

However, the next day, while I was working in my office on 55th Street in NYC, the phone rang. "SHERPA Pet Trading Company, Gayle Martz," I said into the receiver.

"Hello Ms. Martz. My name is Gregg. I'm with Northwest Airlines. I understand you've been having a little problem getting your dog home to you."

"Thank you for calling," I said, a little taken aback. "Yes," I agreed. "I understand KARTU won't be able to fly anytime soon."

"Well that's *not* going to be the case," he responded. "I've decided to undertake a special project for you. I'm going to fly to Memphis to pick her up for you and bring her back with me in the cabin. I'm sure she will be very comfortable."

Northwest Airlines were so happy about the "Pets on Board" program I helped them create that they wanted to do something nice for me. This was beyond nice: this was completely unprecedented!

Poor Gregg and KARTU's first flight had been cancelled, but they finally made it on board an aircraft and arrived at LaGuardia Airport late that night. I met Gregg at eleven o'clock. He was certainly fatigued from a long day of travel, but there he was with my little KARTU. As he placed her in my arms, I thanked him profusely.

"You have done so much for Northwest Airlines. This is the least we could do for you," he replied.

I will never forget that moment. I felt a true sense of pride, combined with the love emanating from the newest member of my family. She fit in perfectly with the SHERPA team at our New York headquarters. I now had a new ambassador to display in our promotional materials and a wonderful new companion. This could not have come at a better time. I had recently acquired Crouch and Fitzgerald, opened up The SHERPA Shop there, and was selling SHERPA products in the New York Madison Avenue flagship store that now belonged to me. As I previously described, I wanted to bring pet travel into the world of true luxury brands and needed more credibility and awareness by being in such a high end, historic company that had been established in 1839. There had already been many articles written about SHERPA, but I still needed to continuously expand the SHERPA brand awareness.

The many national television segments really helped propel SHERPA and me to the next level. If you'll remember back to an earlier chapter, it was around this time that I was booked on Donny Deutsch's *The Big Idea*. He was going to devote an entire segment to the story of how I built my brand, which was just the opportunity I needed. They decided that KARTU would be the dog to appear on the show with me, since SuNae was now ten and easing into retirement.

That interview paid off in a big way. She totally charmed everyone in the studio, and Donny himself was totally smitten with KARTU. That interview gave us a huge audience and added to the momentum in awareness about SHERPA. For years, people came up to me to talk about it, and still do. After that, I was able to book more television appearances, magazine interviews, and other press, all of which helped SHERPA grow.

KARTU is fourteen now. She is still "Miss Attitude." I tell everyone who visits my home that whatever's on the floor is hers. If you drop anything and are slow to pick up your personal belonging, well, from that point forward it belongs to KARTU.

KIMBA: 'True Joy'

KIMBA, a Mi-Ki, came from my breeder in Spain in 2012. Before I decided on a Mi-Ki, I researched for several months. This very new rare toy breed was introduced here in the late 1980s. As mentioned before, they share common ancestry with the Japanese Chin, Maltese, and Papillon. What attracted me the most was the loving, heart-warming traits of the breed and that the breed was very small, typically weighing three pounds. After a lifetime of carrying my dogs with me everywhere, my shoulders and back had begun to give me problems. I needed a small dog that loved people, and especially loved me, but without the extra weight.

I called the same breeder I had gotten SuNae from and asked her if she had a dog that would be perfect for me. She knew all about what would be required of a SHERPA Ambassador. She said she did not have a dog. I was disappointed—until she emailed me back and said, "I have a gift for you!" She had not intended to give up this dog but reconsidered as she thought this one would be perfect for me and my business. This was how KIMBA came into my life. She was three and a half years old, and the day we met we fell in Love. Of course Mademoiselle Chocolate had a name change and became KIMBA. Mi-Kis are renowned for their gentle, social nature. They are calm, adaptable, and altogether delightful. They possess the most endearing characteristics when it comes to their entire personality that is filled with love and joy. Their faithfulness and friendliness, along with their agility, flexibility, and sheer adorableness is absolutely endearing.

Like the canines before her, KIMBA became my constant companion and a part of me. She would jump right into her SHERPA Bag, and we would whisk off to wherever we needed to be. There was another benefit to her tiny size: airline underneath-seat dimensions have been getting smaller for years due to all the electronics located beneath the seat, and naturally the space underneath the seats followed suit. As you know by now, your dog must fit underneath the seat in front of you, so KIMBA was able to travel with me in extreme comfort and ease. Every flight with her was a breeze She was the best little traveler, comfortably remaining in her SHERPA Bag. I could always see her eyes peering at me when I made the slightest move.

Together we attended many travel and pet product shows in America and around Europe. At this point I had shifted my primary role at SHERPA to one of advocacy and brand awareness, so I was spending a great deal of my time at these shows, and KIMBA was the perfect partner. Everyone loved her. She made a positive impression as a brand ambassador. I was promoting pet travel, and people could see an ideal dog for it right before their eyes.

With KIMBA, I once again was blessed with the power of true love and devotion. She was always by my side until the day she too went to the Rainbow Bridge on July 20, 2018. It was a total nightmare, but once again I would never have a dog suffer and she unfortunately had to go. We had shared so many heartwarming, wonderful years together and I am totally grateful for the gift she was to me in my life.

KoKo: The Future of SHERPA

When it came time to get a best friend for KARTU, I knew that another Mi-Ki would be the perfect dog. The first time

I laid eyes on her was when I was working on the computer in Paris and her photo popped up. The name "Chocolate Princess" was under the photo, and I couldn't stop thinking of her. Coincidentally, KIMBA's original name had been "Mademoiselle Chocolate." KoKo is chocolate in color with the cutest little chocolate nose. She was born July 21, 2019 and came to me in San Clemente on December 5, 2019 at five months old. Now she is more than one year old and cappuccino colored. She is a bundle of joyful energy and oh-so cute. She is just a puppy and it takes time and patience to teach and train her. She is a little rocket that flies around the room. She jumps like a rabbit and tires herself from all her playfulness, curls up for a nice nap and then is back at it again. She loves to play with her toys and will fetch anything and bring it back to me endlessly. She is a smart little girl and totally endearing.

Once she is finished with her ongoing "SHERPA training," KoKo will have grown out of all of her bad habits. All my dogs have gone through this rigorous process. Think of it as the canine equivalent of "media training" for a celebrity. My dogs need to be able to possess skills other dogs do not need. They're going to always need to be photographed. They're going to be on television. They've got to be socialized in a way that they can be with all sorts of different people, dogs, cats and not bark or bite. A barking bag is totally out of the question and would never be acceptable anywhere and especially on board an airplane.

If I were to appear on TV, and KoKo were to emerge from her SHERPA Bag yipping her head off or, heaven forbid, bite one of the producers, it would be a disaster. Imagine if KARTU had bitten Donny Deutsch!

KoKo also has to be able to display a public personality that fits the SHERPA mission and vision. We've both have a big job ahead of us in terms of what we're going to continue to do to keep expanding and improving the world of pet travel. I am certain that together KoKo and I will be able to communicate the story of SHERPA and pet travel, sharing what I've always advocated. I know she's up for the job, she is so smart and quick to learn when being trained. Her sweetness, love and love-ability just grows and grows.

While pet travel continues to be my major focus, I am now involved in many other challenges that effect animals and our critically important connections with them. Going back to airlines, the false claims of "emotional support animals" is something that damages the vision I had from the outset. Much of this is fraudulent, and undermines the importance of genuine support and service animals. This has caused some airlines to rethink and even reverse their policies of allowing pets in cabins. This abuse has got to be corrected.

I believe with all my heart in a better future for us and our beloved pets. It's a bright future I envision for *all* animals, since they are under our protective care. That's what Mahatma Gandhi emphasized when he wrote these words: "The greatness of nations and its moral compass can be judged by the way its animals are treated." *Amen!*

That bright future I am hoping for can only be made possible through education and awareness. That is what will open people's minds and hearts. I am determined to play my part in that evolution.

Chapter 9

Strategies for Building a Business from Home

I t is a truism that the only constant in life is change—that change is the one and only thing we can always count on. That is not, by definition, a bad thing. However, in 2020 we have seen a veritable flood, tycoon, and storm of changes. The pandemic. The wildfires. The resultant multiple widespread hardships: mainly health-wise, financial, psychological, and dare I say—spiritual. These have wrought chaos in all of our lives. Of course, this is so to varying degrees, as each life is unique, and each person's body and mind constitutes his or her own ecosystem. How you react to stress may differ from how your neighbor does, or even a loved one with whom you have an intimate connection. Nonetheless, this seemingly endless global health crisis has severely changed life for all of us—perhaps permanently. Where does this leave us—especially those who want or need a new career or business, even though they would be working out of their homes? To me, the eternal optimist, this spells opportunity, specifically for the would-be entrepreneur who wants to build a home-based business and is willing to do the hard work necessary to turn it into something wildly successful. In earlier chapters, I shared how I built the Sherpa Pet Trading Company into a major international business and the name SHERPA into a recognizable global brand. The fact is that I did it at a time when I had virtually no home, no money, and was out of a job as an airline hostess. I hope that this can serve to inspire you to trust your own intuition, creativity, passion for your business idea, and the perceived open niche in the marketplace you believe you can fill.

I shared my highs and lows with you throughout this book by describing many valuable (and often painful) lessons I learned along the way. I want to spend this chapter going over those hard-won business and life lessons. I will include specific ideas for the entrepreneurial-minded—you?—who may be thinking of starting an innovative business and would welcome some inspiration and guidance. I may not have an MBA, but having survived and eventually thrived in one industry for over thirty years, in my case, the pet industry, I believe I'm qualified to offer the kind of advice that might help you. I began at the bottom, was definitely knocked around, and kept on climbing the mountain until I achieved success. Believe me, if I could do it, so can you—and if you have a home, you may be starting with more than I did! Having absorbed valuable lessons about business, people, and the targeted industry, I am now excited to share my own most important strategies with you.

Starting your own business with the idea that it is a solution and fills a need, and further, built on something you love to do, must rest on a strong foundation. Owning a business has many advantages. The process of building it will force you to grow leaps and bounds as a person, develop new skills, and, best of all, meet exciting like-minded people who will form your new community. Take it from someone who has worked in an exciting industry for decades; you will likewise discover when you really get into the weeds. The essence of that field is that most industries are filled with some of the smartest, most caring, and most innovative people in the world. You will find a shared sense of purpose that will spur you to go further and work harder. I sure did!

As I think you know by now, despite all the frustrations and challenges that building the Sherpa Pet Trading Company entailed, it was still the best decision I ever made in my life. Below I've cataloged some of the most valuable lessons I've learned in the course of my long career. Hopefully, they will be useful to you as you make your own foray into whatever challenging industry you choose. I am always learning. Once you have succeeded in your arena, you can reach out to others, form your communities, and share the wonderful, interesting things you have learned!

Do What You Love

When people think about starting a business, they often begin in the wrong place. They ask themselves what will make them the most money. This mindset is doomed to failure. It would be like writing a book and starting with the question "What will sell the most books?" instead of "What is the best story I can tell?"

Let me ask you this: if you could be doing one thing related to becoming a resource for products or services to other people, or even pets, what would that be? Would you be cooking or baking for others? Would you be fighting for rights in a court-room? Perhaps you'd be designing a better garment or running a daycare center or other facility. There are literally endless possibilities for new products or services. Research the market-place. See what's missing or in short supply. See what you can do better than those businesses or services that already exist or bring a needed business or service to an underserved area.

Even when times get tough, if you're doing what you love, you'll always have a deep well of energy, resourcefulness, and determination to draw from. You'll have more than a busi-ness—you'll have a purpose. Finding your purpose is the best thing that can happen to any of us. When I found mine, begin-ning with that little Lhasa Apso and designing a SHERPA Bag she would love to travel in as well as the multitude of cats and dogs; my entire world opened up. You can open up in a similar fashion. Perhaps you already know where your heart lies and just haven't acted upon it yet. If so, what are you waiting for? We have limited time on this earth to achieve our goals, and as I emphasized at the start, the world will always be in a state of constant change. If you are still searching for your true passion for turning into a business or profession, don't force it; let it come to you. You'll know when you find it. Then, once you do, please do everything you can to make it a reality.

Action Means Everything

If you had been in any industry as long as I have, you too would have heard a thousand "brilliant ideas" for new businesses. People come up to me all the time and say, "Gayle, I can't wait to tell you the idea I have for a new business. It's going to blow you away." When I ask them what they've actually done so far, they have to admit that their brilliant idea is "still in the talking stage." That's when I tell them that the idea itself means nothing. Their first reaction is shocking. That's not the affirmative response they were hoping for. What most people want to hear is this, "Your idea is so good that it's going to make you millions!

Of course, I would never say anything like that to anyone. Even if you had the most original idea in the world, it means nothing without a proper foundation. Every business is more work than you could ever initially imagine. The stream of work is virtually endless. It has to become your life, or you will never make it. There will be competitors who will devote every waking breath to their dream, and they will replace you if you stay too long in the slow lane. If you have a good idea and you loiter too long in the "talking stage," you will live to regret the lack of action, especially when you discover that others have actually made "your" idea work.

Starting with a good idea is always helpful. Still, what takes it out of the "someday, maybe" zone is a combination of your excellent work ethic, your execution, your common sense, and being at the right place at the right time. Before you get too excited about your idea, ask yourself if you are willing to commit to countless long days and nights, challenge after challenge, setbacks, heartbreak, all this to maybe, just maybe, reap the rewards of success? If the answer is yes, put a plan in motion.

The next few lessons will help show you how to do just that.

Finding the Void In the Marketplace

When I launched the first SHERPA Bag, as I explained, I created a brand new category. There simply was no other soft-sided pet carrier in the world, let alone any approved for onboard airline travel. Since I was in a category by myself, my only competitors, rather than other pet carrier companies, were airline regulations. I had designed the bag and advocated for policy changes—and I knew that going in. Fortunately, having been a flight attendant, I found an avenue for myself that, at the time, my previous work experiences helped me properly navigate the many storms ahead.

It would help if you aimed to do something similar to your business, which involves careful research. Let's say you wanted to bake and sell gourmet pies from home and sell them from a website. You may think you have the most delicious pies with enticing and original ingredients and descriptions, but do you really have the resources to compete against big companies? Do you honestly believe that your gourmet pies can bypass decades of name recognition, marketing, and brand loyalty? This is not meant to discourage you. I just want you to do major market research from the very beginning and then find a realistic way to stand out. One thought here is going against the grain: meaning that you stress the artisanal nature of your business, the natural ingredients, the custom pies, and cakes you can design for special occasions. There are so many great examples of people that have done remarkable things helping those in need.

Let me re-emphasize that if you don't yet have a concrete idea for your business, try to identify a void in the marketplace—some product, service, or even location that might be underserved or neglected. You might not even be filling a void: just building a better mousetrap could be all it takes. Looking at the current landscape, ask yourself: "What's missing? What are the big brands failing to capitalize on?" Talk to as many people as you can—make the world your focus group! Ask all sorts of people what they don't see in the marketplace they'd like to have. What needs of theirs—and perhaps yours too—are not being met?

Once you've identified a void in the marketplace, devise a strategy to fill it. For those interested in my industry, let's say your market research has identified that people who book so-called professional dog walkers through popular apps may feel as though their walkers aren't properly qualified. They may have discovered, to their great disappointment and regret, that their dogs are being short-changed. They find out that their dog is being taken out in huge packs of 8 to 10 dogs by one walker or by a walker who's been observed standing still, answering his email, or talking on the phone for long periods while a whole pack of eager-to-walk dogs is forced to wait. You look into the issue further and believe these apps could do a much better job of vetting and training their dog sitters and daycare facilities. You could take that information and create a platform that runs background checks on walkers and sitters applying to these platforms—or start a more ethical dog walking business of your own. Voila, you've got the start of a viable business.

If you already have what you are convinced is a brilliant

idea, you absolutely must conduct thorough research to make sure the void you hope to fill isn't already occupied. If you don't do prolific due diligence, you will be caught short, wasting valuable resources when your time, money, and brilliance can be much more successfully put to use elsewhere.

Laying the Foundation

When you begin a new venture, you'll need to set up many components before you launch. What this meant to me, some thirty years ago, was having my mother Connie, a trained accountant and bookkeeper, make sure my financial house was in order. It meant working with the right manufacturing factory in Korea. It meant designing the perfect line of SHERPA Bags. At the same time, a multitude of other things needed to get done.

At this moment, the world is in a major crisis, dealing with a life-threatening global pandemic. The world is a radically different place. Regardless of current social, economic, and other challenges, your business would still need to be guided by the same basic principles. In my experience, a solid foundation for a business is composed of these four main elements:

1. A bulletproof business plan.
2. Financial clarity.
3. Trustworthy employees.
4. A strong marketing and media strategy.

With all the technological and other advances and changes here and everywhere since I started SHERPA, these four concepts continue to apply to the ongoing challenges you will face in the current marketplace. Your website needs to be perfect, your social media marketing plan forged in steel, your connections solid. If you are working with employees, be sure you have chosen the right ones. I certainly made many mistakes in this aspect, and my mother would always tell me to be skeptical, not impulsive. You must make sure the people you hire will be able to do their job and handle the pressures that inevitably come pre and post-launch of any business.

One thing I cannot stress enough: get a terrific accountant whom you trust, and even then, don't trust that person blindly. Go over the books yourself regularly with that professional. If your finances aren't on the up and up, your company will be on the down and down. Be excited, be optimistic, and above all, be prepared.

Keep It Simple

You're an entrepreneur. You probably have a truckload of ideas. That's your modus operandi. When starting a new venture, I would caution you not to let an avalanche of ideas overload one great idea. You don't want your golden ticket to get buried in the snow.

When I started SHERPA, I began with one bag. While many other successful products followed, that bag was the foundation of all that came afterward. I was able to communicate a simple concept perfectly, and that became the cornerstone of my business.

You need to do the same. Don't let ambition snowball into something formless. Pick a direction and stick to it. Ask yourself, "Would I understand this product as a customer? Would I want to buy it? Would I think that this brand is biting off more than they can chew?"

Your business will evolve naturally over time. Let it. Don't stand in the way of progress. The first thing you need is the essential product or service that you can fulfill every time for your customers and always exceed their expectations.

Protecting Yourself

Chapter 6 told you the horrific story of how Bernie Bundt and Louie Lutz misappropriated a significant portion of my business right out from under me. The lesson here is that you must be prepared for anything and everything that will come your way. My experience should serve you as a cautionary tale. I would not want you to go through the pain, sense of betrayal, loss of income, and frustration that I experienced. The emotional toll of such an experience can easily destroy a business. It can even destroy a person. Stress kills!

When starting, you absolutely must take every precaution. Some specifics: safeguard your intellectual property, your business's details, your contracts with employees and partners, and all the other important aspects that starting a company entails. A major component of this cautionary tale is something I failed to do myself: always having a lawyer look over everything. A good attorney is a necessity and an investment that will help you along the way and save you money down the road. It may even save your business. Be certain that every document is ironclad. Some unscrupulous people will try to take advantage of you. Take that as a given. Thankfully, if you protect yourself properly, you can stand up to them and keep what is rightfully yours.

Adjusting to the "New Normal"

When I started SHERPA, most of my business centered on pet travel, pet product-related shows, and other large events. In today's uncertain times, I often ask myself what I would have done had COVID-19 hit right when I was getting SHERPA off the ground. Frankly, it would have been a disaster, though hopefully a disaster I would have been able to weather. The SHERPA Bag was an adaptable product with a multiplicity of uses. Had travel slowed almost to a standstill, as it has today, I would have pivoted the marketing more directly to the home, car, and "around town" products and focused less on airline travel, hotels, etc. Safety at home for you and your pets is paramount in this day and age. You must make sure to be prepared for any of these disasters, unexpected catastrophes, and accidents that can happen in your own home.

Still, there's no doubt that my business in its beginning stages would have suffered massively in this global pandemic. The unfortunate reality is that COVID-19 will impact how we travel by plane, train, bus, and car for a very long time. Things will never go back to exactly the way they were before, and we will all have to adjust to this "New Normal." The parameters your business may have to operate under will be dictated by new social norms, new regulations, and the repercussions in what has become a global economic recession. This is not exactly a bed of roses, but opportunity is always knocking. To be totally honest, I would not recommend starting a business right now that lives and dies in the travel sphere. Far too much is uncertain.

A May 10, 2020 article in *The New York Times* reported that airlines were losing "$350 million to $400 million a day as expenses like payroll, rent and aircraft maintenance far exceed the money they are bringing in. Passenger traffic is down about 94 percent. Then on July 24, 2020, CNBC-TV reported this: "The airline business has hit a fresh patch of turbulence lately, as carrier after carrier reports dismal financial results: In the last quarter, Delta lost a record $2.8 billion, American lost $2.1 billion, United lost $1.6 billion, and Southwest lost $915 million. The hemorrhaging will likely continue, with Covid-19 cases spiking nationally, and the number of passengers going through its checkpoints continuing to dip."

Yet, as devastating as the downturn has been thus far for the airlines, their future prospects may be even bleaker elsewhere.

The International Air Transport Association released its financial outlook for the Global Air Transport Industry, showing that airlines are expected to lose 84.3 billion in 2020. Financially, 2020 will go down as the worst year in the history of aviation. With much of the world closed for business and no widely available vaccine for many months, if not years, it is highly doubtful the airlines will be able to operate as many flights as they did before the crisis. Even when people start flying again, the industry will be transformed, much as after the Sept. 11, 2001 terrorist attacks.

To succeed in this uncharted landscape for businesses, partially or significantly affected by this global pandemic, you'll have to be highly creative and find opportunities that appeal to specific audiences in the current marketplace. Even in a time of unprecedented crisis, there is always a silver lining—a way to make yourself useful and needed. Just make sure you move ahead with your eyes open and be intelligently aware of the changes that can affect your business venture's potential success.

Get Involved in Your Market, Form a Community

It's no secret that SHERPA succeeded because of entire organizations, groups, and similar like-minded, caring pet-related individuals and communities around this country and abroad. People who love their pets have a special relationship with one another. We love to talk, meet up, write emails, and attend conferences. As a businessperson, you should use this phenomenon to your advantage in your areas of interest. Pre-pandemic, I would have told you to go to every conference and product show that you could. Now, of course, they are shut down, and who knows when they will reopen. But reopen, they will, and you need to be on top of them when they do. In the meantime, building an online community is crucial. Make friends through your Instagram and Facebook pages, join groups, attend webinars, and participate in Zoom conferences. All of the major organizations are hosting events live online. Log-in, chat with people, and start to build your brand's identity from the comfort of your own home.

The main point is to meet like-minded people, and perhaps a mentor or two. There is nothing as valuable as a community. It's almost like a second family. Now, more than ever, we need to work together in every aspect of communications.

Being Humble Will Go a Long Way in Endearing You to Others.

I truly know that SHERPA was never about me; rather, it was about pets and the people who love them. I urge you to think the same way about your business. When thinking about your new business and the potential impact it can have on the world, remember to always put the concerns of your prospective customers, clients, or audiences front and center. You will be their ambassador, their voice to the public-at-large.

The level of gratitude I have towards all my wonderful customers cannot be overstated. The many animal lovers with whom I have interacted throughout my career have deeply touched my heart. There has been nothing more beneficial and inspiring than the endearing pet owners who wrote me letters over the years, even to this day. The business I started with SHERPA, the dog, all those years ago, was an evolution in the human-animal bond, which helped me to innovate and serve as a leader of change. Together, we have formed a large worldwide movement to make this a better world for the animals we love. We appreciate how far we have come and recognized how far we need to go. My greatest hope is that my lessons inspire, educate, and entertain you. For those of you—starting your own business—I hope you can move forward with enthusiasm, awareness, and great caution.

I hope I have given you some tools to help you successfully navigate the bumpy roads ahead. Remember that all rustic, unpaved, and difficult-to-navigate country roads eventually turn into high-speed, well-connected superhighways—best of luck in creating or finding what you are really meant to do. Wherever you are, create the business you truly believe in and work very hard towards the life you want to achieve.

It's in the Bag

Chapter 10

Devoting Myself to the Greater Good

I was told a story about an elderly couple; I'll call them George and Laurie Parker, who were given one hour to evacuate their home. It was a sprawling two-story cottage surrounded by lush trees at the Sierra National Forest's edge in Fresno. The Creek Fire was raging—burning and destroying everything in its path. Terrified, their major concern was to transport their two "fur children" safely. They loved Gracie, their ten-year-old miniature poodle, and Lux, their twelve-year-old domestic shorthair rescue. They had never taken their beloved pets anywhere except to the vet. They would put the dog or cat on their lap and hold them for the short, slow drive until they reached their destination. This was a totally different experience; their bodies were shaking with fear of what lay ahead. The couple rushed around in a panic, hastily throwing essential clothing changes, their passports, valuable documents, and other important belongings into two enormous suitcases. Then they hurriedly wheeled them out to their car. After they shut the trunk, they realized they only had minutes left and quickly jumped in the car, preparing to escape to safety.

Just putting the animals in the back seat for their quick evacuation didn't feel right and was certainly not the way they should be traveling. If only they had a type of containment specially designed to keep their pets comfortable and safe for the long car ride and for whatever lies ahead. In a panic, they decided just to put both pets in the back seat, unbelted and unsafe, but far better than leaving them behind—not an option! With their hearts beating out of their chests, the couple looked at each other and quickly drove away.

This incident was told to me by one of the volunteers at Greater Good Charities, one of the remarkable non-profit organizations to which I recently donated a total of more than 11,000 SHERPA Pet Travel Bags, Tote Around Town pet carriers, and other pet-related travel products. Fortunately for the Parkers and their canine and feline pets, a local Greater Good representative was waiting at the motel where the couple would spend the night—along with several other families in similar circumstances. The Parkers and others who needed my donated SHERPA pet carriers were extremely useful to them. I was told they all expressed enormous appreciation—which filled my heart with joy!

As you know, I have always advised people to keep their SHERPA Bags conveniently located on the floor rather than in the closet. It is the pet parents' responsibility to familiarize their pet with the SHERPA Bag and associate it with a pleasant experience. By doing this, their pet has their own private home so that when traumas, disasters, and emergencies suddenly happen, they are in familiar territory. However, in this situation, the exhausted and undeniably stressed Gracie and Lux each went into their cushioned bag without hesitation, first drinking and eating from little bowls right outside, then curling up straight inside for some much-needed rest. The SHERPA Bag had indeed become their' home away from home" as intended.

When the wildfires first started, I was a safe distance away, at my home in San Clemente. Nonetheless, my air quality was affected, as it was throughout California. As I write this, wildfires were and still are raging in ten other states: Arizona, Colorado, Idaho, Montana, Nevada, Oregon, South Dakota, Utah, Washington State, and Wyoming. Watching the horrible events unfold on news programs, I felt that I just had to do whatever I could to help people who were fleeing their homes with their pets and might not have the right kind of pet carriers to use for maximum safety and comfort.

Fortunately, I had a warehouse where I had stored a massive amount of the SHERPA Bags as well as coordinating products for pet guardians. Given the great need, and not only with the wildfires but also with tornadoes, floods, and other extremely dangerous weather conditions that uproot peoples' lives and often mandate evacuations with their pets—I decided I was going to donate the entire warehouse full of both the pet carriers and Travel Collection products to non-profit organizations that I knew would make sure they got into the hands of those with the most urgent need.

I first met Chrissy Beckles at a pet adoption event a year earlier. As any animal lover would be, I too was in awe of the remarkable work she was doing. Chrissy is a perfect example of what Mahatma Gandhi meant when he said, "Be the change you want to see in the world," or what Hillel the Elder wrote, "If not you, then who? If not now, when?"

Chrissy had told me that about 14 years ago, her husband, a Hollywood stuntman, was filming on the island of Puerto Rico. She flew over for her first visit there. She and her husband love dogs and were horrified at what they encountered throughout the island—but most specifically in a place with the unfortunately apt name "Dead Dog Beach," in the municipality of Yabucoa, one of the island's poorest sections. Chrissy discovered that "Dead Dog Beach" was a notorious dumping ground for dogs. When she first walked onto that beach, she saw there were hundreds of dogs running in packs, which was incredibly cruel. Some of the dogs were sick or injured. Some puppies were so hungry they were trying to chew on rocks.

Puerto Rico is an island approximately the size of the State of Connecticut, and throughout the island—a protectorate of the United States—there are an estimated 500,000 stray dogs, or "Satos." Sato is the word used in Puerto Rico and Cuba to refer to a stray dog or cat. Initially, Chrissy found a couple of rescue groups working in Puerto Rico and began volunteering and donating to them. She and her husband also adopted their second "fur child," Boom Boom, from a horrific situation in the Arecibo shelter. That was in 2008. In 2009, she began rescuing dogs full time in Puerto Rico. In November 2011, she officially launched "The Sato Project," a 501(c) (3) charitable organization. Since its inception, The Sato Project has rescued more than 5,000 dogs, rehabilitating them with the highest standards of veterinary care and placing them in loving homes in the mainland U.S. many of the project's missions have involved airlifting dogs before and after natural disasters, including Hurricane Maria in 2017 and the earthquakes that struck Puerto Rico in 2019 and 2020. They also run a "Spayathon," a high volume spaying and neutering program for local residents. While addressing the underlying causes of overpopulation, abandonment, and abuse, they have thus far extended subsidized spay, neuter, and vaccine services to over 7,000 dogs and cats.

Since the devastation of Hurricane Maria in 2017 and the recent earthquakes of 2020, The Sato Project has also expanded into disaster relief efforts, distributing humanitarian and animal emergency supplies, pulling dogs from overburdened municipal shelters with 90%+ euthanasia rates and reuniting families with their beloved pets via the "No Dog Left Behind" program.

At "Dead Dog Beach," The Sato Project has also made monumental changes, including successfully petitioning the mayor for a surrounding security gate, which is closed every evening from 6 pm to 6 am, preventing the easy abandonment of animals.

When I contacted Chrissy, she was thrilled at the idea of receiving a number of the carriers, which she said would be an enormous help. The Greater Good Charities said they would fly a portion of the SHERPA Bags from California to Puerto Rico, where her volunteers would put rescued animals in the bags and, of course, gift the bags to their waiting U.S. based pet parents, as they took them to their forever homes.

When we spoke, she was in Puerto Rico, busily gathering hundreds of dogs to be rescued. Chrissy made a virtual introduction to the people at Greater Good Charities, Inc. They were likewise delighted to accept the bags. They sent several trucks to pick them up, which they did over several days, with great efficiency.

Greater Good Charities is an independent 501(c) (3) charitable organization devoted to, in their words, "improving the health and well-being of people, pets, and the planet." In addition to creating and operating a suite of signature programs, Greater Good Charities has given over $300 million in cash and product grants to charity partners and programs worldwide that work toward our mission." Last year alone, they provided more than $55 million in grants to organizations around the globe. The work mainly in the core areas of world hunger and food insecurity, early detection and treatment of breast cancer, and other widespread health concerns, particularly in women, children's health and well-being, children's literacy, education, and protecting the environment. In the area of pets, they are providing care and feeding of rescued animals in shelters and sanctuaries and work at addressing the root causes of their conditions.

Greater Good Charities, founded in September of 2007, has as its foundation the basic principle that "When we all work together taking small actions, we can actually change the world." That reminds me of yet another memorable quote, this one by cultural anthropologist Margaret Mead, who said: "Never doubt that a small group of thoughtful, committed citizens can change the world; indeed, it's the only thing that ever has."

Liz Baker, CEO of Greater Good Charities, commented, "We are extremely grateful for this generous donation of Sherpa pet carriers that will support our disaster relief efforts by assisting people and pets in crisis situations."

In California in particular, arguably the worst hit by the large number of massive fires currently raging across the west coast and into neighboring states, I knew that Sherpa Bags would be used to safely transport dogs or cats from impacted homes as they are taken to unfamiliar surroundings such as hotels, motels, relatives' homes or temporary shelters. For that reason, I also reached out to the American Red Cross of Southern California. They also graciously thanked me as they accepted a large number of GMInc. bags. I was told that they would use these carriers for wildfire evacuees as well as for other clients who likewise need a way to evacuate with their pets in crisis situations safely. As a Red Cross representative noted, "These amazing gifts will help many people be well-prepared to take their pet along in situations where they must leave their homes in a hurry. Too often, people without a pet carrier are not able to take their dog or cat with them, which is heartbreaking."

I am so blessed that SHERPA became a global brand. This has given me a platform from which to speak about the issues that matter to me. Now, in the latter part of my career, I've largely devoted myself to advocating on behalf of animals, both in and outside the travel industry. This included this list of some of the most pressing challenges we face today with regard to domestic animals. I will do my utmost, with this book, with my podcast, with my educational talks, videos, blogs, and hopefully a number of media appearances, to help in these areas:

- To End Puppy Mills
- To Teach People to Avoid Online Pet Stores and Classified Ads

- To Encourage People to Adopt From a Shelter
- To Let People Know to Always Meet The Breeder
- To Prevent the Glut of Fake Emotional Support Animals
- To Gain Legal Rights For Animals

I always urge others when they become aware of problems that need solutions, to go out there and help solve the problem. Sometimes, the smallest thing you do will go a long way. The welfare of animals must be placed front and center. When that happens on a large scale, we can grow greater in our integrity and quality of life, as individuals and as a species.

I will conclude by saying that with my last breath, I will continue being a global SHERPA Ambassador, even more so when we all rely on digital technology and all other forms of communication. Since safety is and must always be our biggest concern, and since this global pandemic is not finished until we get a vaccine that works, now is not the time to travel. In the meantime, now is the time to spend our extra time doing what we love to do. Stay positive, continue to do the best you can, and, when you don't know what that is, pray with intent. We will all find a way to focus and rise above as we work together, in every way, for the greatest good.

My signature ending was always "Happy Travels," but in this day and time in our lives, "Onward & Upward " is how we will all proceed. Thank you for sharing your time with me in this wonderful community—one we all will continue to grow and build by doing the very best we can. After having so diligently and so tirelessly worked with my mother, Connie, since the beginning and for many years, I know she would be very proud of what I have accomplished. I remain eternally grateful for her help and love. There is no price for unconditional love and devotion.

I hope my story has helped give you confidence in your

own endeavors. If I could start with no home, no money, no job, and somehow go on to build a global brand—well, your future awaits. Please remember what I have always said, that if at first, you don't succeed, try, try again. You will find your way…

About the Author

Gayle Martz is a former airline hostess, fashion photographer, and handbag designer. Her unique vision for pet travel led her to create the SHERPA Bag, the first officially approved soft-sided pet carrier. She revolutionized pet travel by successfully persuading airlines to allow dogs and cats in the passenger cabin. Gayle was the founder and CEO/President of the Sherpa Pet Trading Company from 1989 to 2016. From 2000 to 2005, she was president/CEO of Crouch & Fitzgerald. Her mission has been to change, improve, and enrich the travel and life experience for people and their pets. She has enabled people to take their pets with them wherever they go.

Gayle believes there should be "No Pet Left Behind," which is also the title of her first book, published by Thomas Nelson in 2008. She is currently president of GMInc. (gaylemartz.com). She continues to advocate for all aspects of pet travel, animal welfare, and honoring the precious human-animal bond. A graduate of Long Beach City College, she currently resides in San Clemente, California, and Paris, France.

It's in the Bag

Made in the USA
Middletown, DE
15 February 2021

33827176R00106